page

page

hannah weiner

ROOF BOOKS
NEW YORK

Page by Hannah Weiner

Copyright © 2002 Charles Bernstein in trust for Hannah Weiner.

ISBN: 1-931824-06-1
Library of Congress Catalog Card No.: 2002094024

Roof Books are distributed by
Small Press Distribution
1341 Seventh Avenue
Berkeley, CA 94710-1403
Phone orders: 800-869-7553
spdbooks.org

This book is made possible, in part, with public funds from the New York
State Council on the Arts, a state agency.

NYSCA

ROOF BOOKS
are published by
Segue Foundation
303 East 8th Street
New York, NY 10009
Visit our website at **segue.org**

June 4, 1990

Dear hero,

Well I have just finished this new pages which I discussed
with you important on the telephone   I submit.   glad.
hannah.   perverse period.   Three sections: PAGE (44
pages), ARTICLES (53 pages), SAME PAGE (19 pages). If
you want to disorder them complete you obediently you
stuck confident. So clear I didn't number in order. In order
sequence written honest. Be terriffic. Same written be
careful overconfident historical submit. 116 page sacrifice
omit scared   two more pages conflict singlewoman. Sisclear
be period he laugh bespell beside laughter overlaughter. I
dont finish article speach   two pages sis two pages richard
conflicted. Hannah just suggest there are two more pages
in conflict Indians if you want to see them protect confident
struggle inform let me agree richard. Hope you like this
pages sign obedient like scrawl omit richard please.

love hannah

Hannah Weiner plus object
77 East 12 St. 2G
New York, address until July
then Hudson Guild Farm
Andover New Jersey 07821
summertime august

Hannah Weiner   77 East 12 St., NYC 10003

Hannah Weiner Statement

Mother teaches simple   see introduction enclosed
oh poor   ready   just say it   simple   getting grant
per advisory board   slipped   independent   plus words
seen as i words   capital   some   think   adversary
guggenheim grant adept   why consul   headment   destroy
giving away   crowdog   hint   advers   conditions
adempt   why bill means   political   hurry   five
mountains cost   adverb   boss   why adempt   converse
oh boy bilical   cheap   converse   i claim   see words
as do i seen words   converse   all applications hurry
age perfect   overage   sumit   courage   have   73
poor   oh political   enough   said   hint   encourage
hannah adds her social security disabled number
03   discuss   adverse   capital   920 168converse number
holt   boy   last line joy   converse   submit   gracious
last number   held back   heroine   plus   two   hannah
had   glad   ohboy territory destroyed   sumit   companion
anyone else reading gallup   ferse   point   glad   ohboy
hannah cheats   somone   histry   sumit   despoyed
return   hurt   when   sumit   contray   letter   obey
hannah youve had it up to the line   and one   couromit
hannomit   perverse   plain   ohboy   companion   crow
second class citizen thats what I am indian   crowdog
ohboy teach   mind   by   see   granhalt   mother
speaks silent   and twenty   us clear   sumit introyou
ohboy silent teacher   simple   handle   omit last line

Contents

page

page

oh   I   was finish   a article   youre joking
poor stupid   stop correctly   it wouldnt
hurt stop names   somebody watching feelings
publish this article   whens a period   have you a
publish page   make this a article book   some other
subjects   do you have a reading   well it
cancels it just us   sis it lasts ten days
in our silence   well we dont cancel this girls
page   this little book returns   sis Im
writing return   watch the weather   plus I
get young girl   my   headache sometime
well you had the news   plus this article book
sis it makes it clear conscientious   like this
book   make the fast publish   it says it has
two periods   make more complete   sis it says
something   did you invent   sis it hurts
itself reading   the book   well you get stuck
she puts it in the mail   sentence   because
I fear a mistake   question   dont feel ques you
lost sublime your power   not complete
this sentence page   uncomplete   on this page end
surprise   he hero subject   watchful thats
end sentence   which is it   a paragraph

page

sis I have just adjusted   oh I was me   on
the radio   twice simple   if youre very tired
quit   spiritual   leadership stupid   ol
girl   on the page   what is practical
whoworship   sequences   ontheleadership
continue   on this particular   honest   intrude
page ol stupid   plus included   I was
just publish reading   sis I was article
whats in a article   whats in a board   plus
I have a period   plus combustion   she is very
tired sequence plus   my is this a confusing place
book continued   we judging   how to be a gay
woman   you were eating stretch in a bowl
continue para sentence please ᵖᵃʳᵃˢᵉⁿᵗᵉⁿᶜᵉ ᵃᵇᵒᵛᵉ ᵗʰᵉ
sis have you been street twice an event
cut this page   its all subsist sequence
writing without   they were being cruel
to the older able   dissident writers   like energy
forms   does this page hurt   does the extra page
sis youre stuck on this page   it just quits
someone   likes a paragraph   boy are you stupid
hungry   I was just a paragraph   I omit
stupid sentence structure   I was just a picture in

page

spiritual   blank space is hurry a special
interrupted   on this skip page paragraph
insist a sentence   I was undership   publish
sis hard   make it plain   this poem   public
leadership   ownership condemned   try an
apartment   thats what they say in the   sis
has empty room   someone else likes spiritual crises
it was hard   people practice   have a little
bit   historship   more fun   dont start a
penmanship   quarrel insisted   language
about   insisted about   conquest   on the subject
preference   she it was very hard to be with
try to be careful the leadership   its sis its a
signal   to the elbow   like everyone else
hurry it up a little   space   in a paragraph
Lewhofinish   make this sentence about clear
advice   read pimples   sis I think I was
very careful this subject satisfy   very strict cruel
well your painting   put in the practical   be a girl
sis shes hard   twicesimple   incomplete
informal   untutured   unnatural   it was very
hard put in place to quarrel end this submit
submit this destroy sequence   elegance sentence

page

boy are you playful written   trying to be
careful   writing a paragraph   practice my
dear   on me   have you been a practical girl
sign above   on this subliminal page unlimited
sis sequence   unlisted sis Im
trying to be hardship with myself   more
contractual   unpublish sentence   to be frequented
trying to be more clever with paragraph
yourself included   dont intended   try ended
spiritual hungry eaten   they submit very
carefully   next paragraph   subliminal
context   what is a languageship   unplace
sometime   in a hurry it up a little   the
words are silent   have eaten   being un-
practical   written above   sis please be
honest with yourself practical   very careful
have you been a leadership   subliminal
leadership ^{careful} is often   sis youre in
a hurry   are you being written   some small
pamphlet   describe your language   extra
make it careful agreement place   it was quested
some boys are religious   sis it was
expected   some papers unsold   scareful

page

youre very different   watch yourself
carefully   in the indians undress hut
I am wondering   if the pages hurt
try to be burning more careful letters
with yourself in a drawer   upstairs
thats a submage   Im a written in torment
slowly   dont be slow   in a subdiment
confractural   unbleminate   very careful
with it very complete the sentence period
I was afraid   withdrawn   of with it
have you been unsuccessful   boy are
you being hard to handle   scramble   difficult
with a page to submit form   it was practicable
sis was with hard   thats unexplained
like indians   on the farm three times
four   unexplained   heroworscontructeacher
on this   word above subject   withdrawn
for a complete   I was afraid with it updrawn
dont you please   have you enough subject
matter   have you everyhard   I make
up subliminevocareful   make paragraph
on this page   when ended   as above   youre
have you been incomplete   any digest   thing

page

mother would insist   in a drawer
was   indifferent   to be popular   was
someone indifferent   to be more complete
unsatrefactcomplendifference   please be incomplete
so is indifferent   mother in a drawer
mother purposeful   very careful   straight
writing   was very careful   did you tell anyone
elsesubmit   place   because I was very careful
anyone place   stop language inscripted
sis have you submit language   indescribble
put language playful   mother would scribble
inabove   mother would have you ang   page
do you scinventure   some public   invest
indif it is our aunt   are you scared   have you
any more spiritual power hungry now
to be fed   investiture   mother would
intry to be more humid above   in one
sentenmeansentcompletinsurance   in the submit
complete insurance   mother would be more
careful   because I was sentence please
ubmit on the page   on the page   sis
honest in a drawer please   underwefit language

page

do you have any stupid   just conse
quencomplete   boy are stupid   incomsentence
it reverts inconsequentially   did you write
anymore   fresh fruit   on the table
can anymore you acupdepress   did you
incomplete acuabove   did you committ
ourselves   to the public   sis I was told so
just be silly ol terrible   I was unquilt
mother incomplete   do you have succient
mother thinks unstupid   boy are we
careful insuccient   in a on the left
so is the underfit   on the letter in a
drawer   intrepid   mother is unjust   have
you any quarrels   about you being in with
it subject   boy are you stupid   do you
have an average   thermometer   dont describe
said in one book your name   honestly describe
said in advertise   say quilt   I dont describe
myself   difficult situations   watch yourself
situations   pressure above   dont be acupressure
sometimes page describe curly despair
that was horricontent   please eat a sandwich

discuss acupressure   dont be livid   dont
incomplete   dont be a letter in a drawer
have careful   we have an agreement
we have acupuncture   above pressure
include instructions   have you been
incomon the sentence   complete the sentence
stranger   who tells   what blood disease
acupressure   mother tells interrupted a
story   I was acupressure   did you
feel insensitive   did scribble above
situaincomsenstence   have you describe any
more   be on the subscribe   do you feel
acupressure   on the limit   do you have
any acupuncture   said above   mother
do you forgive did you forscribe   did you
describe situations any   be more practical
carriage insufficient   dont describe
situations any   scratched out with pencil
mother with a pencil   have you any gay lesbian
another   have you subject   did you feel it
yes say did   remember   this page quits
sis its the sentence   blood is describe
that was acupressure   dont surprise

page

go wild stupid furniture   green around
bought   thought   structure   be analysis
sis any physic   gets strength   acupid
go around without   on the page control stupid
go feel furniture   I was cost   sis I had
previous page   my acupuncture   get directions
feel understood   chairs implied   on the
∿∿   thats what it looks brain   discontinue
I got shots   I had abortion   I had to quit
thats what woman writes   just be careful
dissectomy   masturbate   bad description
some people describe   any strength   got
fool acutwice   told   I was surprise   I told you
upstairs   be in a hurry   I dont wear
dont finish anyway   sis I was above
sis it quits   mother would be stupid
get yourself a cage   would have stupid
go drawer finish the article   like sentence stupid
mother was very careful with it stupid dont consequence
have you any   mother above   careful opposite
sis in a hurry drawer   answer any
questions   he in a drawer   stupid drawer
dont complete   just go in complete   sometimes

11

sis please be honest with herself
well write   unfit   very carefully   written
two pages lost   in a rhythym   on the
told   bossit   very hard   sacred principles
congratulations   do we agree   hints toomuch
said it always   write it all down abroad
well we all go around   switch sisters
complete around   I dont wear a sweater
anymore   switch sisters around best
young woman cries for it all   let her name
woman   sis is a special friend   philosophy
breakdown in a winter   go teach   unfit
switch sisters around regularly   someone
hurts   sis he very careful power with
istself quoting   have we careful   power is
enough   I dont describe anymore but
my mind befits   said tues surprise
be brave   why curl it   have you anymore
sis Im being careful with it very nose
very careful   nose extremes   put stupid
day dangerous   feel dangerous   page
day describe   anymore   dont describe   honest

page

power simple   another page   say mother died
simple starpiece   one page   biglittle   holds
the language together   mothers advice praise to
you   sis holds hands   maybe youre stuck
sis this is written in   rich constantly
otherwise   youll get two   sis advice
out of control again   central hall saywhere
see a little pied piper   we tied a little
together   big   spain is simple   we rich to it
put suggest in   my advice   constantly
central conditioning awake   big building
out of control with words   girl suggests
written it doesnt have to be a very long piece
stupid I was crying enough we laugh
constantly   who prepaid   we intelligent
the girls   who speed sis is writing
constantly written on spills   mother is
otherwise   get strict   sis get tough   together
handle holds   of different ages   get strict
in your intelligence   we interested   have
even if you prepared   big listen sometime
sis your   I think I am rich constantly
so   always together stupid only   brothers

page

on the table   bed likewise   bed is table
otherwise   constantly   did I hold
myself together up a little   have you
answered the phone   gets advice   communist girl
peppermint   stay away from the little
I like otherwise   hold yourself together
rich girl sometimes advice   out of control
strong   you had otherwise   bed is
difficult   why watch together   we holds fun
we had exercise   on the floor   was in it
giggles   two trouble   same girl advice
sis its a simple life isnt it   two instructions
give tea   holy rights tight   get   providence classical high
rich girl quick   quickly   stronger
put a letter in the a hurry mail
mother is simple   boy have you courage
I have tried without   fooling around
big linguistic   mother makes samples   waiting
for a simpler word   sis there is some brain damage
much simpler   get off this page gay
sis that was simple a horror
I dont know the last line either   we had it
twice   over the edge   on the table   some short

page

sis table its otherwise   you otherwise
youre young   people get stretch   laugh once
at stronger it   some for others   burntable
kill them ourselves burn newspapers
holy   simple instructions   sis you
get sometimes instructions   like language
articles stupid   sis youre hungry
eager   attitudes   someplace   withgoing
maketable   you plant   make it simple
outside   sis Im hungry with it
poor girl hungry   without sharp
hold yourself together together   make it
often   youre simpler   make it a catch
sis youre otherwise   leaning
put yourself   hands is much simpler
directions   much simpler writing
get off and be quick   on the otherwise
dont forget   hands off otherwise   sis
I had the advantage of seeing it trouble
sis I had trembling   sis a little big
off   but youre sis great sometime
poet continue in trance   much quite simpler
advice   get off the sometime table now
mother would put teacher in trance finish

page

boy if your stuck with trouble   you had a
little trouble sometime   why great teacher yourself
out of control hungry   poet withself   sis your hungry
with it   big trouble in   samestyle its forget
sis I forget everything   sis its just a little
bit of albeit trouble thick   I think smaller
put allowance your in   you can be granted
old great happy poem   you can be granted great
much stronger than you think comment written scatter you
rather than complete   sis its always
together we stay away from the life   handle it much
stronger only in the middle of the line
gently hands   we had a little peace with stronger
much like omit great his we had a stronger little
with name its much stronger than twice   put
stronger I think in   say no is a mu poet stronger
than well you project   sis we class   struggle
doubt   a little stronger   we had a letter purse
we had an agreement once hidden with it   put it in
big print   sis if youre being very together quiet
sis thats line middle simple   dont together sis if

sis its much simpler to think   trouble

sis girl quick   sis its a accomplishment very quick

we feel terrible together handioese its a struggle

we could think of it   we travel print   sis

if it doesnt think boy are you slowly

sis its too much trou skip sentence   sis in my

old age struggle quiet   with struggle it

boy are we a trip   thats where we burst live   thats

a stronger like   switch it around again big little

sis its much letter   sis its much better looking

looking otherwise   sis its trouble specific

sis I think twice   you had a little scribble

make sentence arrive   sis cant you think

we are hungry out much later boy are you

in for a surprise   big little otherwise print

sis Im making a funny little girl   sis its a

big little trouble print sis I had the

advantage of them we twice   sis its much

quicker than english you think to write big anyway

sis I had to think   big together   we hold together

my english is unfinished big book we had troubles

big trouble my english in trouble   get sandwiches with

it   Im hungry much later   much later big little

page

we are eager   sis teacher   marches strict
obedience   enjoyment   sis if I must be
known ^{strict} as a scholar who teaches it
sis words are seen plus happiness if you
preferred   also silence   plus pictures   in a
gleam   half   on the side   like a jacket pocket
which   switch it around a hits   psychiatrist
also dreams   have enjoyed   leave open   shes
scared   obey her signals   some psychiatrists
have dreams   whats to enjoy ^{pictures} in life
big stupi ^{teacher} I was also him   he was only
he was teacher   I was monster   monster ^{little print}

dont mention author of monster story he glad you sandwich

sis made swim   even a no power book ^{thats my monster story}

just dramatizes   just prayer one line simple plus

cast has speach   no power   speak of the simple
sis mother that power was ^{so little he dreams}   he was
an idea   there was no pain ^{more power} that pleases her
sis I made us life simple ^{as a hurry it up teacher} sis
thats very belonging ^{no posessions no trunks} take a leave
they sits   just sister its a long page prominent
I had power with story   very smart people

18

page

sis correct english   I must spell   a
monster is outside   he has no door   speak
only of dont put it on the required   page silence
is a strict   obey   you had strict   at the
door   which   lies   todays   final
space your words twice very carefully
sis signal   dont name I had time   time
obedient   marks   sis is in a hurry
guess whats on time   just be a signal teacher
gives you a lick   sis we like us   sis must
a stamp   I was obedient   I made a
misspell atsme very carefully at the door
signal   sis they teachers some they
make same   sis ob they scream
sis if you sit still and silent it will be
is if youre a friend ^{mention names} they
same teaches ^{plus masters if they obedient to}
the rules   obsolete I write like them   sis
Im scared a little sister intrepud   she
puts language in conclude   correct english
spelling   say words   sis its myself its english
I like everyone else why else not names
put in a little scared   every little sandwich
mother puts in trouble like party

page

too loud   when loud   they laugh when
praise tears   yourself hurt   in tears   some
obey silence   immediately   at first   best go
when signals they language   put in your
own   make destroy signals to each language
in a hurry granted   but my last page first
some say   Im lazy   when my flag
poems were first published I was obedient
thats a line above   praise a strict principle
I was hysterical they the boys around dont punish
them   sis its outloud them boy was I say handle
handle my silence them   them teaches
obey   sis Im rounding about   whem my flag signal I must
meditate   or jump   be quiet   tempted   like curse
acrossthe street ^{wewereworking}   I was obedient pray
signals   at the corner   say men across shelter
do they pray outloud   like that looks I must signal
distress my book   sis I live monster   much obeyed
signals   on the street   get excited   dontacross get
angry   come first   thats what they   handle it teach
at the ashram silly   have you been strict   get silly
stupid lazy ol sis   I meant well   mens obedient

page

leaving a big city   in a tight fit   also   we
have a ruin   some party publish   twice difficult
we leave train   silent   this seat theres much more
bodies generous   on a train speak   because of the
poor condition   we people   sit straight   on the people
front   I was nice to it   did you ever have   speedfreak
analysis with a doctor   pregnant who were you
allowance spent almost before   one peculiar
plus whats in my drawer   like checkbook
heal yourself stupid   on the phone   can you feel
the terror   below the streetline   they feel safe again
downtown big city was a impeccable heal
obstinate   in a hurry   big city   open doors
at night   alone   crossing   the street because
she wasnt in books   enjoyed yourself probably
unsound with title content continue it   renewed
stolen pipe granted quarter   sis if I saw a
million   people dont enjoy   thats what they
think   shop at the store once   advice
solitude   get drunk at the office   sometime
sometimes you understand it   keep only
one I had a shop   small   behind the where
inevident   downtown   sis I called you up

so cheats   it means answers   on the dont give it away
my girl   in this even we study ourselves   by ourselves
answer stupid   origin   once I was before   big
magazine   to old to die for it   remains children
my aunt hurries   in a big hurry   smile   acu-
dont depress   acupuncturist   sis its only one time
sis unfit to say   sis if youre in a bottle on the
shelf hold   drink wine alone for teatime
she also people die   romance   services   gay
reccommended   sorry my girl upset   getting
personal   writing limit style   language   short
particular phrases   like language repeats   who drugs
only science   I had feel   lunch stunk
class consciousness repeats also   among people   and
soblete   information   upstate   wonder   whether
upside you can drive   in the car   mother would drink
its a big problem   driving   alone at night together
happily omit drunk   some name please teases you
I was happy at her house stupid all say home
in the cold   subject   guess whats in a drawer
please wear cold   conscious   I was wearing
some sweater   in ink   on the street corner
in tight   somewhere on the street corner I was

page

people scorn you   are you living across the street
from the grocery store   open   when signals it
bunch of celery please   offend   sis I had
green   so were stuck   with   emobilism
some catches cold   without a sweater on continue
over the shoulders above   like a girl   on the
street   who offers advice get packet   two
stubs   conquest   some drug dealers in the
vicinity   dearest   you had dream   whats
confusion   too many signals please   have you
enough   I was writing all day yesterday   say
enough   until midnight what ever   consolation
thats why big ending   adjust income best   on
the security   have you   I was kidding myself
I was on the security   pass   overthedge   on the
I must go to the month   sis hurry it up a little
some letters dont tell   on the table   in offend   cut
this oldstyle   one line short continue   scrambled
event   of the table   where words open were
I like comments   late at night   when at the
table   stupid   allbedone   I had only   two
sweaters   I lie a little   sis if you feel bad
close   its getting personal again and dont complain
its hard enough   some distinctive person   matches

sis you were beside words yourself with joy
when writing they returned to comfort long
you   and substitute   add pleasure and smile
sis if mother was dead I would break my
tell all   sis spending cut short   dont offend people
a little short thats all period for the rich people
I can offended   I was bought an apartment
close   to they allow it   accross the street
I was punish with it only solitude   sis
I have no one to play with   confidence trick
all beside   getting drawing   boy if you
were strong you would write   only
thats what they think getting hard on yourself below
I had street   as described scribbling   have
you been wearing   sis I seen brilliant show
shoulder   before a tie   in a basket
growing up children very hard speaking
I am allowance fill out the blanks
sorry sister security   youre supposed to be
substitute   a girl   see if its a script
problem   like getting somewhere twice
again   when my mother died she left
at the confidence   her just say enough

page

get your late   old age in order   I just
hint honey   absolute silence in work
like private   say so something about
twice   in the book silly president
and the other one   his name   keep him clear
sometime   I handle him   some presents
at christmas time expected   three children
about five or six   like seventy   get
sis soften   your money spending stupid
spend the half skipping sentence
he sees it in pictures   like crow dog my father
continue   who helps us with them children
because it was cheap   expected   like
dont complete   my father died also
big brave put in sentence confidence
street all religious victory   boy are you cruel
in the street junkies   offer handshake
giving up white structure   said see in pictures
mother likes gentlemen   put in praises
allow us children   expected   touch together
someone is indignant   continue children
two short together   put generous in   hurts costly
someone put wrong   say dishes in   put popular
like writing again   strong she captures it

page

mother likes you clean to tell confident
guess what heroic struggle allovertheworld
without voices   like me   sis its a big
trouble to learn   will important once in a
letter file   I just remembers   somehouse
on the field   also mountain   which signalled
from the boys   say men   complete under control
thats sentence   I dont mean arms like abroad
I mentioned it munitions   which I bought once
only for a friend in need   bought arms once
on the farm   where the boys struggle   over the initials
be with them   dance twice and my wife might get white
like she long hair cut it dreaming   say alone
if you watch the weather faint also   I want out
this yesterday   buy me meat   just for a lamb chop
combined   blood clots safest   meat untold   blood
pressures low indeed   say orient delicious
some cleanse   raise your blood pressure you chill
every day sleep   I personal night give up your allowance
anyone else ginger   I give up speaking   be clever inside

page

sis my   broad belly   in   the   kitchen
last line first   ok   I was apples in the kitchen
have you any bore   what a lesson   to be a
subject ^{over a manuscript}   enclosed   enclosed
research department   guess object whats on
the screen   phone answer   she is required
to publish the publish   because of paragraph
paragraph   page   same   on this place   piece
one page a day remembers someone   who is else
why writing paper   so its at someone   buy it on
the street   precluse   remores   decluse   import
offent   some publish   its an argument stupid
publish the manuscript   offself   that she was
dead when arrived   overhead   brooklyn says
if the manuscript was published   she cameabroad
with winter   all alone at last   sis if I can
get that same published   from awhere artist
make him pure get the poet quicker   step solidly
makes hes a boy   glad he refuses   strictly abroad
invitation   name goes sameboy both   guess why
the boys in a tight   sis sorry to name it   put publish

sis   its instructions   I just dont want to
write about the dont failure   the struck
stupid   on the level   sis shewill reliquishes
the form one on a page stupid one on a page
mother would eat an apple stupid and   end
the whole thing understand   complete and sentences
mother was primitive   she was over eighty
when she died also bedroom father   bedroom
quilt   she also alone room   when cold   flu
sis if I get sick in home   I cancel my trip before
my read my family stu four girls   one aunt
oh understand aunt yells   at the outside
sickgirl   bedroom   upstairs   many beautiful
pictures   I do see pictures   sis strategy
insist   controls it   sis she was
almost apple lover   sis I bitter food
frequently   sis a bitter smile   someone
else its a great experiment with
my friend   who has three children   stupid
sis youre being an experiment for the content
subject about yourself   it was conscious
thought   overmind   read the will   I must
cancel it   for some names sake forever
boys cancel the office   ending complete

page

boy is it beautiful   from the hills
boys energy   flash   by power alone
sit alone   the women come to gather
talking   you make sense sometimes
great leader born   sis uphill   they upheld
strict child   knew from her father   I
would speachless   heal other childless
children born   bab   I heal other children
by touch   someone suggests it   I refused
to do it stupid   just reccommend distortion
diagnose district   mother was a baby
called diagnosis   distrust your childhood
sis explains it   bye bye explains   expected children
two children   like   by the hand   to touch
the baby   diaper   he was tumid   I had
out of control with it   stop sentencing steal
Id obligate   sis stroke healing   with
vinegar purple   outside strategy   childhood
this was it   sentence intelligent   upset
child who couldnt talk   talk about baby
healer   your life is granted too stupid
were you granted   mother   granted
sis the boys laugh   at you current stop
laugh go broke   I was a both   understand
dont mention the thorns either   blue stepping
over the fields at night   non skipping   sis
it means no thorns were met by the feet enclose

page

some healer now suggests publishing   she wants you
to do before it for go broke   she   sis almost
you had a stroke   with a   clockwork
superficial   extremes   sis I dont
intended   name makes me strict thats him
writes   until   dead at 90   guess what that
means   same to him   very old man stupid
ver old when disguises   same name is old when
he dies   horses reccommended I am 88
same as mother dies   old tremble   three
big mistakes in granted your life stupid
like husband unwilling   like children unleft
and the publish was unstuck   dont publish yourself
some piece describe illness   it wont get published
the fast broke   on the list stupid ol dear
I didnt write early   hurting us children
forever   without   grandchild obedience   strong
woman stupid   sis Im forgiven journalism
on the account   Im provided   in the
subject   my childhood better   teachers
always alone   I was always alone in the
back yard   where wirestrap   forbidden
my child   because you jewishmy girl
radio   sis I temper tantrums when young   hang in child
in go stuck   youre wild   dont publish me print

sis I had another story complete   childhood
I was a swimmer   alone   along shore
very difficult grow   to be alone   with
sis it was very difficult   speachless
but I was a student   some party
included   some indent score   I was hiding
in it   beloved strangers   on the walking
mother would quit   lying back   duality
make paper   this paper included   president
kennedy killed himself in his car   without
protection stupid   like chief who
dances bushes   they surround him openly
gently   in the officer   no one protected him
like indians hint   always driving   his
ended   and his wife tended   two little
children   they were horror   but they four
sis I was four years old when I left
for my backyard   sis   its almost the end
when its time   sis bullshit   publishing
some aunt   has required almy
aunts name   sayname   was it ever
changed ever   was she female born   lived
with my other book   when I was alone she

page

some aunt provided   sis I dont
remember   who died first   because both
some get winter   beach   hysterical   died
close together   when august mother ill
mother died september   remember at the
beach   forgotten   written in language
in other book spoke   under duress   childhood
please your aunt stupid ol silly   romance
included   never had children   close to my
childrens   sis she was never dont worry
about children   who   obey their parents
quit   sis if youre honest   continue
some   storm   comes   I was belligerent
I was beggar also   on the 4th below
insulted   my aunt came   have a permanent
she lived in us   separate room   like
jealous   she cared for my mother stupid
when breakfast   I came playful   headaches return
spoil   sis I was spoiled indeed but restricted
because I was female   old age stupid
my very clever girl   wonders about it always
sis it happens next   turn page   classical high providence

page

your poor aunt dies should follow   page indiscrete
I had my diaper on   dignity   sis child
hood experiences   collect poison   I was dressed
very carefully   tucked in at the neck warm
dont spoil it   belligerent I was when I
over forty   forgiven   childhood remembrances
stay awhile   smile ponder   other   being
alone without mother   often very difficult
she was punished   with behaviour
sis let alone college was a little jealous of me
because I was bright   frightened off
when I was eighteen   I was outspoken
when I was tried   I was going to this
college then   when I was   special member
of the big group alone   for a year at   my
dont home again   put yourself on the line
as everyone does   at the college separate
sis I was offended her   the college excited
when   graduated top I had   with
sorry about   I didnt suffer   I read books only
sis I was only illiterate   every novel
succession   everyone became tonight   four
make five of us   sis hold hands up   everyone magna

page

sitting   go breath   I tried hard   twice
enough   feel hard   sublimate   house
subject   filling somewhere   speaking
Ive been a mutation   sis shes a
little hard of hearing   dissociate   sit
calmer   sis solitude greetings   along
my child same   obligates   sis she has
a hearing problem   difficult to diagnose
with some musician who is a leader   very strong
picture   reccommmended abstinence   for childhood
and to be very old together   mother would
work   putting the short   have you enough
penetrated   hairlong   boy are you forty
boyson is obligated   havent divorced   who
are you   say friend invited to bewildered
who genultimate   refuses to holler
unless language prohibited   guess what
a scholar is   better   if you were joking
he was fake fall and promises   all is
playing   now on the shelf stupid   horrid
these little girl   havent any nice
buttons   we prize   boy   are we careful

page

mother was very careful with her
childhood   grew up dress suddenly   clothes
she own   plate   worker as same as me
making clothes   sis blue beads
sis she wore dress under her coat   long
sleeve   like me   to touch shoulder   very
hard writing   she before it   she made
clothes   she wore long dresses   in our style
sis youre wrong   in the eighties she
stop writing   twospeed   who was tender
as me   loved another behind   his wife
kindly invited me to show off another
person indicated   plus person   purses
put down   someone bothersome   for not
calling   when I was touchy   neighborhood
calling back   put her down for her memory
forgiven   sis if your in shock dress
very carefully   toucy   cant spell   sis
touchy mustspell   figure it out   bust
in the touchy   sis very careful   opening
sis it was hard to be alone with
condition   obsolete   careful   we granted

page

albatross   who navigates   have you   under
famous line control   have you an different
half   long   two days struggle   say
disgusted   if you open the boys
mind   sis it after the struggle   that
I hurt   I was touchy crawly   havent
you any money   I am walking on third
to be a villain   except   it becomes shit
thats how person writes   somehow
downtown street   in the black window
crawling with windows   overlooking a
backyard   there are four buildings there
without trees   walk back a little   side
collapse careful   youll be energy field   youre
stuck with it   high   flying   around
the mens shelter bridge   stupid girl
who was high   early seventies window
had   heartache   watchsun   difficult   two
complain   heating problem   difficult
stairs instead   some drink you were poor
very sunny way   I mentioned pick bums   they
walk past skipping   I was drunk on the
complete   street   camp   sis   around

36

page

go before spilling   sis I never again
I was machine   so I had a cold
unfold   upset   unbent   across the page
I was stopped   every minute   subsidize
hard core   eventual   no weeks   sis   exact attitude
the one   who name   cares not   remember me
Im like other people   big people speak only
now if I liked the name   who is bent
machine spills event   everything machines
uneventful spill   have an upset   beach cries
tohold   sis   mother would cry a little
have you untold   song brother
sis it fills up   follow the details   somewhat
hint   embarrassment   comment please
sis I had to read peoples minds for it
anywhere   so carefully   pretty girl someone
else   likes   who   she lives in a place
Im   always there   someone places   in a home
are you believing   in a friend   who cries suddenly
someone places   forgodsake forgiven
sis   Im very carefully educated france
everyone changes everything once around

page

for coffee I drank   and some liquor   bad boys
follow me   someone else helps   where did
you live   bread at the corner baking   which I had
the boys   sis I had fresh bread every day thats
for a cancer problem   and no white food either
how many doctors write   do explain   cervix
complained   examined   but problem
breast cancer absolute   sis if I had low
metabolism   all my life stupid   hungry
from eating too fast   boy was my brother mad
sis it was a trick on his mind to obey
mind instructions   when angry   very
careful with it includ   I almost help   say
Indians   wave of a hand from a big   who
names   power entailed   for a week for a while
until it was   I sat for a week for a while
until I was healed   somewhere drove along
sis I had a lot visions power then   sis
I give bliss away because nothing but
recovering   the leader   sis the some Indians cured
me   for listening thats all and I white   big
leader lives south except for his garments now
sis they save his clothes   for a year now

38

boy are you oversized   big enjoyed stab
to the chest   got him where   not to the $^1/_2$ inch
youre cloth strong from the chest   big
died   in his late very his wife explained to me
sis the baby calls stra that suffices
some Indians who know me give me old
sis they thought I was because I fought
pipe   delivered after period   which I almost
you poor dear explain   explain children
like hurt   theyre visit some place   some
plains   children vote   let the children vote
please   sis thats conference   peace
I dont have any to write power left   except
sunday   thats a leader stupid   furniture only
sis doctor I had severe depression   my friend thinks
ever before 6 months exactly to know exactly
perfume   sis I told them early   september
that year remember   some page spoke the author
answer forbade exact date 7   believe the
July out of control   I had to listen to it   four
months plus   subject excused   sis
big guru does write about myself first
because I was learning to show   sis dont
hint spoke is a great big book thats all

boy ^{dead} have you an intelligent mother   stand
say you had a stroke immediately   something
letter destroyed   sis I try very hard to
please people with obedience   make mother
very happy   some leader same book with hasnt
read quietly enough for feel   she stopped
sis I dont spread   above name spells nice
dont you wish you were a nice girl somehow
name above read august   speak above
have you a very strong mother   broke even   well
she died   sis I almost died myself a mental
reject   in the someone   sis this says goodbye
sis we last names only   just say goodbye
mother dies slowly put it on the spoke
august page date included   mothers death
I was surprised at it   both sisters include
in   sis I was laughing it   dont spoke anymore
sis thats all finished   now change style
problem interlude   dont introduce yourself
sit and still   quiet   until same month
mother is dead   already sentember
stroke subsided by drinking also thats all
superior   mother lived a long life died slowly

sis I repeat my sentences   write mother
death   I believed   sis I forgot the dont be
ashamed the date   and wasnt slowly coming
sis I didnt said elsewhere any more words
sis I didnt see I repeat myself see words
ohmyspell anymore   like I want   sis I
cant cry   very caused because some people gave
me   what   sopills   so cancel your
arrangement   mother writes always it down
skip pills   some doctor   three years
silent good any Indian would after death
sis long period any Indian would signify
I mean specific   sis I like my message
changed word   got cleaner   went bill   who
neighbor   good neighbors   someone else would
write   I wrote twice about mothers
sis she was getting old cant you tell
cant the dishes   getting cold again   my
mothers book shows   sis I was sleep again
so tonight   my light night   so I went
my mother   sis she died slowly   as older
some pretty girl older   very hard woman too stupid
mother dies older   sis tuck   get exercise

mother would like a broom   mother had
a cherry   poor people ring the doorbell   say
where you providence lived   clean   modern
lets chill it us   somewhat   summer cancels
address   let it go the beach rich   sis she sees
you have on object in mind her mind
also sequence letter   mother dont tease
would write   herself a letter during the drink
sis we had together   some celibate
abroad is becoming an independent state   stay
celibate   sis I always said it twice   once silent
sis thats gurus correct answer   once more
mother would like you to thoroughly sit once
in a while stupid   for ecstasy   sis if youre
in a great big hurry youll read   my car is afraid
of you   transp mind   obsolete   we know
the difference   true or false   distance   overhead
scream at us for the felt   sis that was quick
your father was a period   sis he had a
manuscript   about life of childhood   dont teach
with him   father is embarrassment   older children
please   under the underwwater   make him underwriter
make him courage   make him please   get the underwater

older woman language   sis hurries   sis
she had a great big book out of house   otherway
round   otherwise   hurry it up a lit   well I
explain why   sis she gold has a big june
at the end nobody comes   some book finishes her
sentences   thats me   sis shes selfish to her office
off gate   sis its tragic fate   mothers remorse
went into a building   we came into it   like an
old woman   we stick together   sis old days
sis its a hard woman   march is very
separate   unless   expected   have a
condiment   pray hard   joke   tender area below
the button   boy are you lying about it   trying
keep lying   well you have your safety belt
have you ever had a rich car   sis I lose
a seat belt in the car   sis thats pamphlet
written   every drunk is beside herself   mother
returns her calls   sis someone teaches   upstate
sis you didnt have an planned pamphlet
some hysterical people call it that   once more
one more tribe   one more bullshit evening
who had the advantage of me   someone elses address
sis someone else drives   make sun afternoon
sis she feel attractive   boy beside   and afternoon

page

brilliant child has a hurry   sis
practice on her jump   sis she hurts jumping
sis told her twice   skiprope jumping   along
sis I was working inside   describe your
moments   sis I cancel this   sis skip
necessary   under influence   sis I had a
baroque influence   sis thats cracky
you solve problems otherwise   known
downtown you were hungry   you were living
it green   people speed   about the evening
somebody calls very no wedding   late yesterday
like beautiful   like working   we were hungry
at liver problem   very journal please   sis next
year I write   as I please   like office   boy did
you have a terrible mother   who is living   upset
sis telephone say youre broke   over the envelopes
mail keep track away   every bullshit artist
has me over to dinner stupid   would   everything
oh skip skipping   sis mother skips a gay
point   relaxing   over the underwear   how
many people   some dear friend has a bed   sis
youre saying skip reading also   sis we weaken
sis mother would add   young poets live let communist party live

sis I cant write a novel   anymore until   sis
death   someone else   suggests it   longtime
overweight   introduce sis its a low
keep pills off   and waking   in the
morning   have you finished your novel
sis I almost ended with a picture instead
Im a woman   big church   the season is
skip   ended season   sis mother
would smell cocaine   come child has it in her
it keeps her busy on time   sis thats
someone who has   she shouldnt be working
she shouldnt after fifty   has name is it
hands in pocket   put it away   smell
sis I mean man   someone   who is in the street
without a car   name has snow in her keep secret
like older   who is in Indians   someone else
would like a trip   offer   sis   she has wisdom
in her coat   that means high   sis everyone carries
cash in the dont say hang continue   clothes are experience
sis thats what they city say in autumn   mother
says nothing   sis   old words in sequence study
boy do you have the advantage poetry style

sis we had a wisdom for phoning   sis
ok messages even event two hours long
sis big reader very jealous certainty
very reward honesty   sometimes he heard
very hard manuscript   following orders
from different people   and my orders
sis invents   some interesting   below
enough   christian someone explains every
thing to you cost   plus books   plus energy
thats how we describe it field   only   rises
plus a trick   lost   get the past in the mail
sis silly question   guess what it costs
sandwiches extra   for food enough   try harder
eat easter   sis mother would come   pull
that cord   something else solution   to what problem
what finishes promise   four pages go   everyone
edits   everyone was in ^{say practice} some communist
childgirl   rushes   mother finishes   make it
thursday   or alternate   sis hint please what
to do for yourself   when your mother dies
sis I had dying to me   so it was said say where
remember the forgiven   the pages   sis I spoke
promises afterfall   in this winter   if Im alone
seen words finishes happy myself   I must explain
just take a chance add addition   see words although
I had to handle it like someone   please through
make yourself a poet   sit strong   and please

articles

oh   my silent being   honor   struck
win paragraph   under   put paragraph
hannah youre stuck   under telephone
which page   which struck   under
silent pretense   sending allowance
oh boy silly   underdrawer   simple
hannah   put complaint   underdresser
send ron silliman letter   let it be
content   underdresser   send sandwiches
be prayer   let sandwiches   under control
silent   obvious   struck   being   hannah
Im struck   watch   beverycarefulwatch
under   Im   repeating myself   underwear
some silent   oh forget   being   put on page
answer questions   who is director   correct
sentence   obvious   youre struck   contract
dont hurt him being   consent   put in
drawer   stay silent   quick on   street
say tender   some teacher   say scrawl
put in letter   forget advice   get extravagant
intelligent   some indifference   mother
puts her pen in   quick letter   complete
some teacher complete be quiet subtle

sis title article

seen sacred object   say page   under control
when alliance   it repeats itself   under george
who sunders   who understands   civilization   get
stuck with it   big learning stick   thats
strict obedience   hannah obvious
written silently   under control   say handle
mother would youre proud   say where
hurt   sometime   sis its under control   say handle
audience   thats finish   dont complete heroics
mother would word take out   says obvious
get control   hungry   someone   underground
picture   in your mind   uplit   like
professor   keep clean   send drawers
send company   two lit   like confidence
put it in letter form   keep secret
put in another   tender   publish consent
with drawers   put in a line drawers
mother would consent   he honestly   quit
unless consent   whats a trick   give advice
under control   whats silently   seen withdrawn
two years under control   sir ron copies
sis listening   send him his open
sis question him listening   open letter

sis title article

sis strict intelligence   copies indifference
spelling underwear   spit   sometime
hannah he has underdrawers   sweaters
complete   unlimit   send drawers
what repeats sentence   what jokes
what spending   his abroad   alone
strict company   teacher   keep silence
under influence   hes afraid   youre stuck
begin again   like twice   perfect
beginning   he relaxes   keep understanding
keep perfect unfit   keep pictures in it
obvious underdrawer   hannah youre stuck
written   in   written   underwritten   offside
keep silence strict   under control   like
church   where read   silence   youre
struck dumb   silent editor   like someone
when understood   keep copies   go abroad
once   offset   punish yourself   understood
big   handle different   send article abroad
send another letter   big brother believes
hes struck   underwhich   hes control it
subdervise   get control of it   public
information   put it on the   publish sent

sis title article

get performance in   get letter in   get france in
send abroad letter   mother sends letter
dont hurt feelings   like obvious   put print
your delicate in   silent teaching   like
letter   your instructions   sis its letter to
subject   where publishes   he starts   quarrel
about listening   dont hurt hannah   put
youre struck dumb   silence letters   dont
forget   sign off your obvious   like hurt
twice   get repeat   youre hinting   great
publisher diminishes   sis it read aloud
keep company   go abroad silence   thats
teaching   like mother taught daughter
like twice   put in letter   hannah it
repeats itself youre stuck   strict   around
little   list   youre afraid   getting lit
underwear   unfit   some complete their
complete   underwear   boys ice   drink
he hints it   hannah seen stuck
words again   publish seen   put in allowance
sis get off the sentence   where underwear
some silence   put drawer in   confidence
must sign gratitude   finish complete   hannah
youre stuck with silence   strict   confidence
complete edition   sorry   complete education

sis title article

like letter this   put teacher in   bring
string   put ronsillimanletter   strict control
youre stuck   grandmother like teacher   he
under cut it short   publish   honor   stinks
under control   repeat   get language article
regrets   certain   complete afraid   unlisten
complete structure   getwithit   he sandwich
says somethbread   your friend   get license
driver   forward   hannah he gets his
letter in the mail   teacher   also like
brush   silent teach somewhat embarrassment
hidden   quick   like complete   understanding
swift kick in the direction   hannah hes gentle
mother publishes   just cross   make neat
letter scrawl   complete edition   just let it be
handle youre stuck   send magazine some
confidence   quick   send ron silliman
guesses   put your silence in   your letter in
say white   be careful white   dont publish
anger   gets hungry again   sign letter
put offside   ronsubject   letter   regrets
send newspaper   go abroad again   hannah
he repeats himself   drugstore   some
different   typical   some instructions
some pages practice each   hold silence
together   publish   confidence   youre
struck dumb   contract   omit citylive

sis title article

sis mother regrets sign   pretty tricky
sign honest   listen publisher   youre stuck
with silence   seeing words   like switching
forehead   understood   like twice   confident
silence otherwise   boys we stuck   get
magazine publisher   somewhere   put hannah
say drawer   ron silliman underwear   gets letter
sis stuck page again   twice   sign letter   ron
suggests hesitates   comfort   like grammar
mother would put it conference   may ended
some angry   handle conference   say stuck
honor   grab   somewhat   some tender
sis give place to him   put hannah in
again   youre stuck underwear   get drawers
in   hang   before   get unfit   beware
finish   laugh   get structure   like silence
give in to him   send letter abroad
mother laughter   hannah destroys letter
get off the youre stuck hint   silent controls it
sis complete end paragraph   laugh   put sentence
get structure   put silence paragraph   put structure

sis title article

put strong   take eight stuck   get
silent   get instructions   get company cruel
thats happy   pray content   six obvious
when control   hannah comment   eight
when stuck   keep silence strict   keep
order publish   send this magazine this   send
friendship   kinship   handle hannah
put silence in   twice again   thats stuck
same advisor   complete twice   angry
just   hannah hes hungry teacher   some
quarrel   please freeze   some danger   some
stuck   some just publish it
quarrel   gets send original drawer
sends silence   quit seen   instructions
anger honest   ron silliman thinking
much simpler obvious   get drawer
hannah handles it differently   just put
children in   get wise   silent   underground
forever barking   keep strict   like obedience
hannah dog   hannah he laughs at himself
making say struck   big delicious   get off
the money   put problem connect improblem

sis title article

complete flight   some embarrassment   copy
letter   your strict silence better   send
copies later   make teaching otherwise   get
cruel   send offset   getoffthepage   complete
end sentence now   send somewhere   put subject
embarrass   compliment   send selfish   put dog
in   teaching   letter   he gets in mail   big
trick   hannah   complete silence   send his
money back   his cruel   hannah   hes cruel with
power unless courage   get off with it   some
teachers   english   beware strict confidence
keep repeat   send mail   your instructions
put happy in   your gaining happy
mother abroad would telephone   send
argue   put hungry letter   send silence in
send this somewhere   get wise   be buttons
press   suggest   tender   some unless
letter   he quarrels it   mother angry
sis its finshed   some trance   spending
boy youre in a ticklish position   sending
abroad twice   sending sentence   some letter
seen words with scramble   seen obey   send
silence   instructions   seen material
mother finishes   mother would put her silence
in at the end   complete the silence twice

plus title

why do we argue in silence august   some
guilty   start article   touch   may date   should
some poison   relieve   starch   some city
believe we country   said miracle   toast
dont blame with the screen   so obvious   doesnt
tell truth   dont hurt   screen   always obvious
strict silence article   write pages   some
embarrassment   why be cruel   ugly   obstinate
hannah thats obligated   heat   some scream
always two pages   indifferent   best august
technique   give away secrets   some words lie
not exactly correct position   mother obey
contract   get wise to television   some correct
when advise   often bewildered   some screen clear
mother like scientists   some parapsychology
call   or obey   indifference to public get scared
difficult   get name doctor   hes opinion
almost scared   dont explain   when he died
knows more about drugs   when he died
correct position lying   so explain correct
position   lying straight on back   movie   screen
must be intelligent   gaining political   strength

plus title

mother would worry about herself til her
scratch it honest   keep scramble   office
insult   wear sweater   my suggest   alone
graduation   very delicate situation   see words
on television   must be correct program
like news hurts   some correct   difficult
crossword   some obligate   dont believe
phone cord   hannah thats hard believe   keep
secret bullshit   why struggle   feel guilty
when I die I may be   some indifference
to culture   bruce andrews talking   have
you history   why sentence   put in mail
always indifferent   some person enclosure
doesnt spell correctly   like audience
more power   old screen   see whos
testing you   always   please speak
indifference   name special   always windows
brick   upstairs   dont follow people
some words   please dont complain thursday
some silent   get sick   where   some
healer correct   stay at home obsolete
continue punishment   describe very obstinate
by very careful   street obvious   when scared

plus title

mother goes crazy   heard   earlier
just scramble voices   like obvious heard
some breakdown   scrawl   how many
pages left   popular   keep silence
put it on prayer   office   sis struggle
answer its passage   too holy strategy
get structure   pure silence   two objectives
follow   seen instructions   seen orders
like follow   be an instructor   give
lessons   teach brilliant   like satchidananda
always   handle people   some seen pictures
some television silence   sis it keeps
writing   boys I think its hard
bewildered   at the corner   keep silence
strict   be office   handshake   be
difficult   some spread legs   like down
very hard   watch television   obligated
seen words explain it   teaching very hard
strict silence obvious   to hear silent
mother would keep instructions   put it in record
keep off screaming   get file   unrestricted
bewitched   always contact   careful indeed

plus title

plus indians included   keep switching it
around   keep healer straight   sis kisses
obey stricture   somebody always explain
two words   in a hurry   publish surprise
dont get hurt saturday   dont complain
tuesday   special bravery   hannah its
honest   commentary   big brave silly
subject   have you trained obvious
sitting   pretty obvious   handle central
intelligence   some judges suffer   keep
secret obvious   handle   poor example
youre home   scream   honest   big
editor clean   sis scream history   doesnt
complete education   some teases   watch screen
mother likes it   some screen   words
obvious   printed   just spelling   big words
directly across   prevent spelling   hannah
youre historical   plus pictures   in your mind
some strict   people around   hannah screams
whatever are they power   use intelligence
sis thats the scratch it out   big powerful
people   not with strict   sorry embarg   somewhat
embarrass   some culture serious   get quilt
hannah its all done   new pages   luxurious

plus title

hannah you have proof your mind words
works forget   some scrawl indifference
popular heroics   work embarrassment
get off the corner   keep lights youre page
honest quit   six dumb enough   finish
indulgence   keep chapter   doesnt grant
kid   apply   somewhat   hurts   dont be a
humble   screen popular television   just
children   say youre hurting scramble
her words   honest   like calm   get straight
dont let on bewildered   sis keep silence
forever punishment   keep delicate   sis thats
trick us   some screen   big words   always
say program   must be Im sorry   bewildered
get across screen   destroy confidence   keep
tricks   bewildered   dont enjoy eat   bring
hurt   correct silence   seen words always
beginners apologize   some correct english
you lost honest your program   now confusion
still be silent   keep confidence   dont
struggle   downstairs   always bewildered   say
officer   keep struck   get off the page in confidence
keep control it   street   get excited   cross

plus title

big miracle   hello tuesday   someone   sis
continue   switch stations   some policeman
hannah switch silence   watch policeman
some structure   very hard white culture
drop culture   learning strict   culture
like article said writing   to be heard
some culture   excellent   like books
like broadcast   who details   get with it
some officer   stay protect   why some city
telepathy   parapsycontinue   he learning
tried to officer   feel guilty   some subject
get off with subject   interferrence   speak
youre kind   much obligated   distance
apologize   some invented   big simple
unders   switch teacher   some subject
complete objection   hurts silence   street
sis keep calm officer   once in control
hannah it keeps repeating switch   like
gramma   who is it   big judges   under
control society   big culture obligated   sis
some indifference   awkward subculture history
silent   underground   some culture repeats history

plus title

boy are you in correct position   always sitting
boys tough   watch program   see if
correct   see words on television obvious
some like protection   you go history
very obligated   disgusted   obey instincts
mother wouldnt hurt anybody   just
scream   boys   big screen   just
juncture   big article   big difficult
decision   big decide   opposite   mother
would scream words if she had to listen
to it forever   put in forever   tough scrawl
hannah its complete   like flat on back   when
just words seen   problem   correct
position   why protection   believe us
hannah its obvious like   youre
protected like other   some bewildered
mother would scream if she couldnt laugh
put obligate   when intelligence   keep screen
keep lying back   mother is principle
always protects   like richard   sign off
mother likes screen   watch silently
seen words in opposition   give away secret
opposition   two feel guilty   embarrass
two hazard   complete   indulgence   scared

plus title

big abroad   always content   central
words   PRINTED   see honest   escape
BIG PRINT SACRED INTELLI   very plain
seen awkward   police difficult   just scream
someone hurt   skip page   big history
hannah someone teaches us silently thats
all I say   hannah mother said no
big pages confess   congratulations   difficult
hannah thats police   skip page agriculture
thats angry   always polluted   some magazine
always digested   just suggest   skip water
hannah well you struggle   handle agriculture
some difficult   always grain   between
polluted   great scientist   say bread
always untuted   big conference hungry
without bread on   switch subject   big
history dies slowly   mother is in a hurry
correct position lying   complete education
classical   say when educated   before war confidence
get clean advise   hanna   omit obligations
stay straight   calm   lying   keep off
get culture embarrass   get clean   mother
born and educated november 4 1928 curtain
740 curl   obstinate   clean   hannah honest
clean page   keep strict   two die   influence
say white   pages   correct   spend   spelling

control   words seen and heard silent teacher

obey all your orders ol instinct should be at the top of the page
get along with it   get along with drugstore
plus telephone indeed   ended substitution
sis quarrel   some harrassment   public enemy
sis discuss   transference   you heard it
some enjoy particular   some details   embarrass
we quit famous   darling   sis it hurts
spelling   otherwise   other power   many
submits   on the calm   subordinate
two officers   like policeman   mother strong
gives advice   teach   when women   since
together   poor somewhat   black instinct
boy are you taught sincere   someone omitted
somewhat because   big pimples   overteen
problem   delighted   big suffering   on
the house   stars continue   with dedicated
please page structure   sign hannah   youre
stonger   beach beginner   teachers alone
hannah youre stuck audience   big brother also
intelligent subdervise   boy are you almost
sis it gets hysterical at beginning   mother
finishes   paragraph   skip silent   confident
your almost   have in tears   complete double   sacred silence

control

sis put your careful   sentence silence
structure in   calif   complete subvision
we control it   very carefully   underwear
some speak   some changes   we weaken
easily   get pages   handsome   get culture
off   we silent being   sandwiches   people
boy are you tired   very public quarrel
sis just add in one line line please   correct   submit
have glorious   what subscribe   answer difficult
someone cord   speaks difficult   guess   who
teaches   brushes   quit silence   my brother is
honest   pig contest   see correct intelligence
get off the in a hurry   indians pretend history
talk arguable   say hungry   some teaching
honey   put practice in   some sitting   have
you telephone   see serious illness   comfort
underground   get cross sentence   get me abroad once
people guess honest   have you telephone
substitute   some beware   somewhat control
guesses which   teacher silent   have under
dont continue   some lesson   strict abroad
intelligence   quarrel about   learning teach

control

somewhat embarrassed I write   put ticket in
travel abroad   like a   seen silliman
road   honest contest   problem undergr
some error   hannah youre teaching
seen tuck   sudervise   handle   submit
someone gets wise too much   tough laugh
have you plural   put suffering women
women older   below average speaking
some danger sign   get off the page limit
ron otherwise disagrees with information
plus hint   get kisses   put stronger in
plus meeting   quit problemonthestore
some white people   afraid power   white
suppose some children background   white
teaching   central   work telephone   callmebe
his farm   central intelligence   be clever
put it in obedience   some brothers   defy
silence   power control   advertise   put
public in   switch it around family
sis quit kidding youre pregnant   somewhat
keep writing stupid origin   stuck again   blank
me teacher only   unless embarrass   say page
we agree on tear   you must be silent through

control

put in mother likes furniture at the end
sis discuss literature   second silence tough
people laugh   put submit encourage   stuck
alone   put problem finish   what article
say farm   say untight   six pages lost alone
we strategy   comfort   older teacher   picture
get glasses   only strict   pure education
some present colleges   put independent
brother teach   somewhat   hes unconscious
like present brother   kisses me around
sis balance   put sis strict rules indians in
broad   against culture completely   hidden
like state   excellent   some excellent
get excited tease   someintelligentwomenare
you had count   prevent illness   stay
alivebe   white independent   who city be
about somewhat instant   bewildlike indians
somewhat   power   please forgiveness in
some truck   like power spent   hungry
money spent   be in a pickle   scramble   house
dont be instinct   agriculture   hysterical
offsensive   quiet   omit sentence substitute
get off the page silent   mother gets hint
put struggle in   silent strength

control

sis its power struggle with spelling
put indians terriffic truck   put teacher
sis quit kidding yourself youre   hidden always
some silent indians truck   beware of stuck
put me in a ticket   like brothers alone
somewhat embarrass   finish with spelling
please people collapse   over eighty perhaps
somewhat dying   untilundercontrolpower
strict intelligence agency   put power in
again   put independent   some silence in
two pages lost in a hurry   be comfortable
when   older woman   take   amountthemoney
sis embarrass   some greeting allowance
sis underwear   mother puts fit tender
study language abroad   say stuck   in
a hurry   ron what pickles   teacher silently
sis hinting control   what obedience indians
some beware unfit   some independent
skip page intelligent   some provcorrect
seen telling   leave strict silence
correct page in your silence dear language correct
sis structure   subculture   dont be in a great big quilt
brother hurts correct his a little

control

sis struck language   intelligence   put in
angry   get public audience   see control it
power controls excited   when scramble
great historical writing   someone agrees silence
quit trouble   stay underground   live longer
we stretch   put across structure   hannah
we omit public   understood silence
be   some teacher alone   big provcontrol
technique   youre stuck   samecontrol special
say died   lateinherlifeofcancerlive
strict liver   put in anger
someone is scared with provcontrol
we agree   silence   sis ticket   count
your money   get around quick   delicate
get providence under control what im
saying   big city allowance   get wise
drugstore   put danger alone   sis sign
off   withbettyindangerlife   big trick
some title   go abroad silence   suggest
himself   brother when   when I die
maybe   putindangerlife
quarter past eight   big strict exempt
put title control obvious when hungry

control

independent alone   big handsome   score
sis its a struggle to write completely
some language   putbrotherhimself
some article like   publish penmanship
kidding quietly   punishmentsentence
some obedient   driver substitute   provide
quite providecorrect   story   make cancer
strict   boy do we embarrass   provicenter city
say where born   hidden   pastculture
strict audience   same silliman controls
quarrel ended   some intelligencein
put poor   suggest   tenderness
we feel guilty writing   because silence
instructor   believe teacher   slow
embarrassquit   written hidden   like darling
have you enough against lying down
strict sis culture   im sorry please
submit paragraph   lesson silence
instructor provi   get central object
get struggle in   sis yourstuck with great laugh
paragraph   enclosure   submit with the
same intelligence language   put alone
mother would put in another line saying shes correct

control

mother died cruel in a hospital bed is what lecture
seen words control with it should be the comfortable
sis strict intelligence agency should be the end
hannah has quarrel put in elevator language
be glad with strict   seen control   argue a little
sis mother skips a page   when intelligence in
sis youre much younger woman when you write it
believe in us struggle   submit paragraph ending
mother would put in her ending paragh silence
sis sentence ending   above letter   some stronger
quit struggle   put independent indifference
sis quit above   some literature   like state
quit writing above silence   seen attendance only
sis its much stronger than you otherwise
give comfortable lesson   quit writing page
strict brave control   be silence intelligence
mother would control balance   get off with it
page silent get indians strong   please submit
get courage with it   sis strong indians silence content
seen under control some embarrassment feel
pages up   sublimate   quit darling   hannah fasting

control

hannah mother would control with it poor
silent being   last paragraph speaking
send stricture above   lesson continued
leave blank space   unfinished article
someone proviculture   very delicate situation
get tricks off   bewildered   some cause it
providence central angency   why be
long paragraph   purple ending   so be it
strict silence intended   skip paragraph
above   be special horror   big spending
describe   average intelligence   sis its
hard of learning   sis intelligence proviagency
controls   when spent   believe luxury
bedding   some kisses   fequent embarrassment
strict culture   omit providence
some kick you hard enspelling   quick
seen ending   somewhat ticketsif youplease
get ticklish in a hurry   spending
abroad luxury   since auditor white
hannah has a stroke   with black control
get off kick   hannah just dont audience
some handle   quit   put struggle sentence
some black embarrassment at the picture

control

spilling the beans   quit control with
it   hannah speaking   over eighty with
subject   ask subject   control objective
teach attractive   somewhat embarrassment
mother has author   somewhat
historical   put speaking lecture   witness
quit historical   coming   overflower
being gay   opposite   confidence
once lecturer dies   strict serious obvious
silence   subdervision   city streets please
get courage in   lecture   historical
bewildered   handwritten   subembarrass
brick   trick   some learning indicated
just touch off   be brilliant   editor
same blame youre stuck with
intelligence   someone understands   us
tricks   silence   someone stuck   underallow
slightly religious   beware   bewrepeat
slightly undertaken   learning sacred
be intelligence agency   get off the
page quickly   just finish article space
unlimit movement   strict intelligence   quit
luxurious   sign complete   name   spelling
like dictator   hannah Im spelling two words

control

put your embarrassment   strong woman
kick black embarrassment   someone is above
mother kicks   hard embarrassment
quit culture   submit   writingindeed
someone gets hint with   intelligence
sis kicking hard black   always suffer
first   be intelligent   be officer strict
say police on public   be confidence in
some strong culture black   get off the
subject with   black culture luxury
kick   kick them in housing
get strong lesson   let black believe culture
indians along   abovestreetaboveembarrassment
quit lecture   somewhat strict   audience
sis audience black   culture subdivises
spend literature   spelling   kick intelligent
let black history quick   strong
be strict be blank   quit culture guilty
forget which   mother is off the page
submit agriculture   some people struggle
with it   stuck   kick   trick   spending
sis quit kidding yourself over spelling
black intelligent   some embarrassment

control

someone guesses whats wrong with our
white advertise   put it in   culture embarrass
hannah   thirteen pages   submit historical
strict lecture   bigindifferencetopublicopinion
get struck   somewhat indifferent
mother cont watch continue   picture strict
just careful   just joke   get off the street
silent   white careful   be brave comfort
describe picture   somewhat   advertise
get stronger women   put teacher advertise
silent undersubdervision   complete
hannah stops pictures   sis quit seen words
paragraph   just length   hinting   paragraph
long   repeat stricture   mother spending
someone gives destroy   luxury   big
somewhat   put yourself kicking hard
somewhat subside   strict hinting
hurting on street   white sentence glad
bewildered   mother would imbolent
hannah its strict silence subculture
8 converts obedient   quit obedience
quit culture hanging   sis mother would
put in brave teach lesson above

control

mother struggles eight pages strong
quit audience lecturer   strong captive
strong   we believe in it   obvious sitting
black history around   let culture history
silent like around   teacher   unlit
some pictures in your history   strict
some structure   repeating sentence obedient
some publish granted   get white culture
history   sis destroy get yourself granted
white jewish obey   be subdervise   sis
quick   strict repeating   agriculture
mother was struck angel   history
orient   otherwise   subculture advertise
continue   break above   black people
switch culture   power get off the
page submit agriculbeginning   strict
this month   keep history subculture
subdevise   strict   sis
honest   be gay   overculture   embarrass
mother overjoyed   quit lesbian honor
please father   somewhat strict   beware
of the dog   mother hints paragraph
mother gets a dog for a lesson

control

sis substitute embarrassment   sis culture
willingly   give instructions   otherwise
get culture orient   quit culture obedient
someone strict   like obedience   child
when   black culture   sis its trick
silence understanding   be traveller
sis quiet youre struck dumb lecturer
please gratitude   someone collapses
number offset   beware page culture
somewhat ticklish   get off the opposite
sis strict attendance   give lecturer
standing   mother count pages   sis
quit submit   sis twenty pages long
submit agriculture   quit lecturer
history   some please   despite advisor
black history   some history lesson
guess   what licks   sis destroy
cultureembarrassment   very literature
smiling content   be black   like official
please funeral in   count your pages twenty
give lecturer   strict control   garage
give strict   slight   embarrassment   people
mother gives hurry   blackculture

control

sis it counts its pages twice   twice belong
mother obvious   count your pages
silly old woman   get controlwithit
sis twenty conflict   count backward
some obvious   put struggle in   indians
indifference white   trance   bewithitalways
power contains   sis curtain   apologize
three more indifferent   count aoplogize
give central committ   omit structure
give advice   control glad   oh boy
are you silent intelligent   mother
would hint twenty pages in silence
sis   stroking   just appointing
get tired writing   advise   bit stronger
hannah advisor   control   learning
strict dont complete   sis culturehistory
we repeat childish   stronger   historybackwards
get think   between   sis   culture
black subculture   history   limits
mother hints stroking   get obvious
mother puts lecturer in   someone
silence   quit advertising   advertise bewildered
some structure   some complete   some understanding

control

sis strict culture repeat   obedient strict
teaching   like agriculture   subculture admits
youre getting historical   twin towers admit
getting culture in   strict intelligence upstairs
very hard bitter   keep control liquor
very hard bitter   send company license
submit lecturer   when   angry abroad
someone bewildered   sis its hard tough
writing seen words   intelligent
please be officer   like target
police   be in street   obey black teacher
someone offended   say strict abroad
get lecturer hurry   abroad in history
get silence boring   sis youre culture
history   quit lecturer strict bewildered
college education   listen   complete
pamphlet   strict education   like
history beating   some agriculture strong
dont hit impudent   get lecturer history
some hint lecture   controlswithitsorry
sis getting strong please get twenty
please please   get off the page hungry

control

seen words with it control   last page
sublimit   control punish   control officer
black continue   begin period   thats
coincidence   we meet twice   some
strong   get street advise   wise street
city district   when wild   go strict
silence   strict silence off the street
dont hurt people   congratulations   we
quarrel   dont upset   repeat subculture
strict enjoyment   get history enjoyment
let street clean   some block   some
control   seen agency   get strict remorse
when controlling intelligence   special
laughter   sis quick fifty twenty   get
history strong   like we black officer
opposite control   when strict writing
holding confidence   get scared history
black culture indignant   some history
correct   bewildered silence   some
lecturer   some audience   quick
some healer advise   get stronger women
youre stuck with honesty   cruel person
quit history repeat   mother likes repeat
get strong   get page   get handsome
sis trick   beholding   some letter

control

mother would say seen words at the beginning
strict subculture silent   embarrassment
just twenty pages long submit twiceagain
hannah mother would repeat wording repeat
strict culture   strict   hannah quit tease
two hours long please   count pages opposite
hannah mother would put in her opposite
see black culture ending   subculture interested
quit writing my believe   silent understanding
boy are you hard enough   learning strict
hannah mother confesses she writes contact
sis quit lecturer history   abroad instructor
please leave us independent   you are struck
dumb with beware   quit teaching   obvious
put your page instructor in   please limit
twenty scandal enough   get stronger women
put black in again   around the table twice
quit kidding university   professor understood
some blank silence   put stronger women in
sis youre repeating   somewhat intelligence
get off repeat the page obvious   one week
content strict   go abroad correct   will
out of control agency   pretty handle
please put correct instructor in

control

put ending content   please honest control
make people laugh counting   sis strict
obedience   one works   slight huntry
get county counting   black   back pages
count like lecturer   plus twenty   two
please hurry up   quick   like teacher
count   please be very careful
obvious struggle with agriculture
quite embarrassment   give lick off
let tranquil be   unlimited   finish the
page   mother submit the frontier
church   where stop   reading   like
picture   abroad   when sitting silent
writing history lesson   please objective
white control it   plus   somewhat
teacher destroy intelligence   history
when limit   youre stuck writing again
must listen   blushes   get fifty quit
long   over   silent   sis quit
writing schedule   silence lectureabroad
silent black silent   one month abroad
silence   sis strong confessor   count pages
backward   simple ending   strict confidence

start comfort

mary has comfort in her   straight
women onthebeach   comfortable   beformit
mother wise   clean children   in the bush
mother resents it   clean clothing   wash
control you   hurt it   mary subdervise
women get with it   permanent   take
twice   please omit   practical   hair
mother blesses   control   firedanger
make draw   simple   undertable
pictures   youre kidding   some pictures in
breakfast histbehave   have table on mother
resents it   please put on a drawer   quit
kidding   hide embarrassment   we drawers
hannah keep silence often   swim stroke
some description   ending   farm complete
with children   be quick like a laundry
hannah stroke   please joke in yourself
drawers   mary unfinish   we quiet
unfarm   particular   seen pictures
someone sees pictures in a embarrassment
some tuck   begin stroke   hannah its
empty strict   just complete ending mary ending

start comfort

mary has blush   continued   stick in
drawer   mary publish   infrequent
some ladies   old   senior   walk slowly
hold hannah   be little   children strict
say new jersey   licks   under   some trees
big lake pond   under   some beach
for little children   sis strict   no pond
umbrella   on wet   pavement   we stroke
just under   breast   swimming   go
flat   mary reads   tender   hannah its
august we like   brother wild   come
suddenly   harrass   big hammock   bad
breast   brother is stuck   finally   put
in july   very hot week   underwater
please trees   some underwaterlesson
underlawn   please drive   complete
ending   it takes a week   to swim under
in   get address   disappointment   mother
would correct   address   important   seen
tired august tired   see otherwise   put in
journal   shes reading   august quarrel
save your friendship   strict at surprise dinner

start comfort

some unlock the door at night   week
dont stars alone   we guesses strong
tender buttons article   seen words again
twice article   six children   save organ
I meant damp   hurt   riding begin
it hurts jump   be a friendship
dances   she finishes   brings
collapse   with intense   sensible
mother would finish   two   friendship
sis it kids her in her silence hannah
stop writing in strict someenjoyment
cross out page   forbidden   just compliment
mother forbids journal   clean drawers
mother likes it   no coal   some describe
same friendship names   put   cute
in   some socks   bewildered   she tells me
silently drawers   she hints blue   me
other   wear five   bring complaint
hannah it hints silent teacher
silent talent   on the beach   some teachers
some   big brilliant editor   takes home
salary   put in stocks   I mean furnitureexcuse
get bosses lift   undress   comfort
sis ending please   silent comfort instructions
put page in please   comfort relaxoncomfortinstructisilencbroadcomfort

start comfort

sit silent rain   please next month
mother wants a dress on the underwear   undress
put in   white   bring together
sis dont mention names again   boys
laugh   get stuck in   twice remember
tender   please give in altogether   write
backward   please teacher   submit
carefully   somewhat awkward   put in
very carefully   boy are you uncareful
mother leaves pages out   underground
submit language   tear article   some
women strict unusual whereveritbe
mother pleases   very carefully   get
instructions from calling   whisper   dont
imitate   lunch   mother gathers   sis
pretend   one striccomplete   printed
someone complete   underwater   mother
handles it   someone attractive   see dress
big blue   see other   get touch   dontmentionnation
sis thats hard spelling   put in touch
ending with   cut it same   please touch
mother would put her ending on her page
mother concludes on the last page finish artisubdevision

start comfort

please be quiet sister   take it down   under
confess   wet   paint   in the bottom
sweat   tele   speak   we comfort   reading
hannah handles it like cross   silent
women   please continue   subdervise
control   please   guess   whatunderwear
please   white   hannah   youre stuck
again   five pages   quit hysterical
laughter   broom   sis thats honest guesses
she subdervise   she cleans house omit
omitted   granted   she pleases us
quit subdervise   guess what limit
guess women   people praise   get off the
page   mother ensorry   incompleteending
sis quarrel   we limit ourselves to each
other   big principle   silent teachers only
sis describe situations   before same women
she happy   all summer attractive
pur her belongings in   carry a quilt
abroad   that takes silence   mother hints
guess the phone bell   just finishes
please name please page please laugh omit
sis mother pages finish   mary hints other
she turns about   mary subdervise hints two pages

clairvoyant writing   june 1990

secret alteritive

mother is protectsilence give allowance sis
youre teaching advice get nine pages in
your excitement big drawing nasome
surprise some technique keep silence
strict lecturer big teacher audience
stop scrawling give advice in stricture
mother get off the page suggest augallow
allocutitshort put publish argument
very quickteacher stuck quaint
sit silence lecturer big agreement
get off the page silence big lecturer
stuck big page mothers stuck advice
put richard begin plus lecturer
say lecturer big silence mynconfuse
prowhere get publisher see picture also
we lying taking life big pictures in
big angel big stuck city name lecturer
sis sister switch around agent
my name big boss hung around
hannah just say almost abroad structure
give suggest put long in some particular
last line destroy abolish please listen

secret alteritive

sis give advice structure   some lecturer sunday
six pages long twist   mention lesson
big teacher spending   strict writing clear
big structure   douglas has furniture
youre stuck   give advance silence
structure lecture   sis silence publisher
sis leacutit   provcutcity   quit city also
get home   big silence   get writing in
take life granted   some provi always   big
teacher like pet   some scrawling editor
some lecture teach   put structure bless
sis complain above   silence seen above
elegance   some embarrassment allow
always spring   big elegance   big complete
stop writing plan page   seven pages quit
some money difference   quit shocking
lecturer   read silence   famous like
quarrel   big study   give structure
some plenty   above words   clean page
always polite exercise   big excellent
intelligent get off the page quit   instrucintellbrave
last page silence   quit writing against
sis lecturer   put abroad   get structure repeat allcut

secret alteritive

awkward sentence give in   blind   send sentence
mother gets strong   give punishment writing
big scrawl even   get publish   quit hispunish
put your name on it   page   some lecturer
sit silence structure some quit
put establish instructor   say quitteach
boy are you intelligent   mother reverses beware
sit attendance   give provicut audience
sis structure silence   mother likes   scrawling
some bending   give teaching instruction
mother is struck page together   omit
mother beware   ten pages   better advice
get lecturer scrawl   bending lecturer
give advice scrawl   men   brother strucambiance
poor instructions   give spelling   lecture
mother hungry   you bitter much broken
put clearest   give hungry   put tease
put allow   get lecturer abroad silent
go someplace   black   white   practical   omit
youre sentence   give blind   put above silence
give blind people structure
give ending paragraph   last page embarcut
dont quit embarrasstechnique   quit writing page
mother would put silence in suggest filling
sis it teases practice almost finish page

secret alteritive

give ending big   surprise twelve pages
when hungry   get allowance   big tender
spending   quit   big tender   specutitshort
skip quarrel   quit teacher   some
instructor   give audience   instructor
parade   big spending discuss   sis big
discourse   say instructor   very heavy
big brilliant advance in   stop
scolding   peopleadvancein   quit
advancing   give spending quitperfect
quit intelligent   people guess intelligent
horror   intelligent page seen
with repeating   instructions   blame provi
put danger awkward   youre given quickly
be careful practical give practical obedience
get off the thirteen   honest page twelve count
please name strict party please better
mother twelve would obey since teacher
always better hinting   give advice
instructor   get heroic   get transfer   some
spending cutitshort   big trick   more
spending   youre getting   quit perfect
same page   mother likes lectureraudiencelecturer

secret alteritive

put historical   his cruel   you were allcutitspend
youre stuck   big truck   big sister abroad
mother spending big tender   push awkward
put buttons aggravatetelushoneaggravate
please publish more   twicestucktwice
sis keep writing   anotherpage   off the sorrow
tense   instructor   finish conflict
tender   go alone embarrassment
put youre stuck   sis give in to
him always   get stuck off the page
sis listen mother   please publish twice
some quit   writingmaterialwritingabroad
sis spending youre stuck   big lecturer
strict   best lecturer   get teasing quick
get someone stuck   both pleased to structure
both clairvoyant   specialiststeachinsbalance
such subject drawing   spending conflict
correct   strict companions   big expensive
cant aboard   readbackwardsreadspecial
just suggest   importantaudiencegivein
mother would spend her last allospending
on her lecturer   big youre stuck   some
clairvoyance   teachingallowancespecial
one more line please   specialinstructor

secret alteritive

remembered punishment goes abroad   silent
best tears in again   always   get luck
sister   cuthispageshort   always get leader
severe punishment   always punishment
sis attractive   end lecturer abroadcorrect
sis teacher   correct teach   get technique in
subject   quit on page instructor   rich
people abroad   get silence sister   get
off silent sister   intelligent people
please include   some subject advice
put advice instructor   get wash   teacher
sis mother spending   get stuck your in
put teacher in   embarrass   silenceinstructor
best teaching silenceinstructor   best polish audience
skip lines twice above   put in reverse
order   book scandal   some together
we always   some lecturers advice
please finish page silence   page silence
mother likes seen words to be the spiral
put in silence instructor   above correct
sis director   put in silence above
mother lecturer stop silence teach
mother puts page silent above teach instructor silence agreabroadcontrapun

title kick hard subject interferblastruc

anyone equal to us can be   pagrgraph suppose you were an agent
equal language to us   put it around
some poets   BECLAIMED   strict
silence   send it   ABROADCONSCIOUS
suddenly   STRICKENCONSCIOUS   material
hidden   SUBMATERIAL   put delirious
in   some hidden   PUNISHMENT
you were stroking   BREASTING   mary
is   GIVINGAWAYHUNTINGAWAY
secrets   anxiety   SOME PUBLISHER
ol boy quiet   SOMELECTUREgetoffthepage
signal poems   obedient   OBEDIENT   get
strike   PUBLISHGUARANTEE   omit
have you strict   sincere apologies boyfriend
put your answer in   LEAVECORNERONLY
put associate   OPENDRAWERPLEASECONTINENT
put eager   ENCOURAGEMENT   mary
D I V   C O N T I N Usmile
pretty LONGERHAIRBREATHER   omit
name   PRETTYGIRLONGERROSES
sis contempt   PAGETWOCONTINUES
ask richard   CONTENTMENTindiansilently independencultureshift across
page silently across   indians silently   page silent two

title kick hard

put courage in   drink twice   office put confusion
put yourself in a garage   LIVINGQUARTERS
stupid and silly   INDIANSBEHAVEINDIANS
and see what it means   slightly
embarrassed   raise BREAKFAST OMIT
continue page   correct   CEREAL OPEN
employ better   get off the page obedient
get strict   add to the pages obedient
just   EMBARRASSMENT   stick to
your garage   sleeping   WITHOUT
alone   SUBMITSUBMITENCOURAGE
hannah have   sis if you feel poor you
will feel tired   sis john   braveryexcited
sis hes elegant   TEACHERENGLISH
put him around   gather someone
great teacher   somewhat embarrassment
hannah somewhat   THACHERTEACHER
hannah   SOME   TEACHEREMBQUSTROKE
hannah same technique please
have omit   SOME JOHN   SKIP   mother
please consider position   hungry angry
put book away   DECEMBERONLYJULY
excellent page   constructionemploy
sis its silent page hungry add historical omit

title kick hard

boys communicate   extrapublishassociate
sis its content somebody   EXTRAVAGANT
mother hurts   CONTENTMENT   pleaseembaquit
mother likes blue   mothers contentment
sis   honest COUNTTENPAGES   believeinit
hannah mother tells you corner   story
be continued   SOMEWHAT   CONTENT
BIG   WRITING   CONFUSED   COMFORT
give   DIALING PHONE   BE ANSWER
someone   EMBARRASSMENT   sisitsanswer
big punishment   scare people   instead
have ugly   PUTPLEASE   sisblue
please   PLEASE CONTENTMENT   please
suffer   somewhat   boy are you lucky
to have a mother   put solitude in
sis consulate   BRILLIANTUNTERINSTEAD
stupid girl finishes   sis embarrassed
mother likes   CLEVEREMBARRASSMENT
cover your heard   see CONTENTMENT
pictures   see page only   get off
somewhat embarrassed I write a dont bother
give in to your mother please silent with
bottom of page   seenwords   correct

title kick hard

sis silent editor CONFUSED SUBJECTIVE
somewhat hysterical I always blanket
some material SOMEBLUEMATOBEYUGLY
some steal BLUEPENPENMANSHHIP
big journey EMBARRASSMENT get off
the   have you a DARLING sister quiet
sincere doubt BLUEQUILTSUBJECT
argue abstractly SISABROADTOUCHER
put yourself in teacher LONELINESS
subject INTERESTED behaviour sis
its strict IMPERFATURE embquit
some teacher strict grown up confront
eagerness SOMEHANDLEQUIETLY
sis mother PARADISEMENT give in to
PRACTIONER consent DOCTOR since
ALLOWANCE come above complete
single strict EMBITERenemquit
perfect PAGESCREAMINGPAGE hannah
say quilt OMITTEDABOVE strict behave
mother consoles TEACHTELECROSS
somewhat embarrassed I teach across
beware subject transfer contract permit object
sis telephone please correct page corrected

title kick hard

poor quit   mother suggests pages omit
put clever in   PRETTY   DRESSUNDERDRESS
private   SOMETHING UNDERCONTENT   sis
subject entirely   quit   put only in
page complete   sorry embarrass   some comfort
bewildered   SOMEFRIDAYAFTERCONCERT
very tired   SOMEDAYAFTERNOON   prizeconcert
six objects   boys ticklish worried   some
saturday   PRIZED   six honest content
mother pushes   DRAWING   complete sorry
sister ending   COMPLETECONTENTMENT   abroad
conscious   even hug   big CLOSURE
sis entertainment   sis saturday afternoon
closed   SILENT   ENTERTAINMENT   some
what   blank space   TIREDEXHAUSCOMMENT
omit strategy   COMMENTDIFFICULT
pretty drugstore   COMMITAFFLICTION   silent
advice   be   ARGUMENT   sis   ticklpunk
CONGRATULATIONSSTUPID omit
mother is   PRACTICABLE   hannah
dont   UNPRESSURE
confess   sis confess honest clean enjoy
I enjoy writing   confused opposition

title kick hard

sis pretty page please   silent subject
get off the page transfer   get subject some embateacher
enjoy   mother likes a big blue bed and
you save hysterical   get off the hysterical
GET PRACTICAL   put enjoyment in   SOMEADDRESSSOME
plus jacket in classome tears about complain
please elegant please elegant tear it confuse
put preface   ENLIGHTENSORRY
mother quits   GET YOUR PLEASE
hungry embcatchcold   sis put your
folding in   subject   SILENCEBREAKFAST
be humble transfer   problem offset
see english   GETPROFESSOROFF
sis if you were a great big intelligent
writer you would watch a period
put in   TEACHERADJUST   somethoughtonly
poor   teacher object   sis quit embarrass
entirely   GETOFFTHEPAGESISTER
put money in   classical
get strict   some citywhere
mother would spend   sis get historical
put spending teach   and spendingcomplete
mother would put in her last comfort

title kick hard

SILENTinstructcompinstructor DISTRICT LEADER
obey   silence instructor   luxury
building   EMBARRASSMENT   some
leader   being   brought   toward
extra food   TAKELONGERABROAD
some teacher quick   LIKELUXURYBUILD
sis quit kidding   ALLOWANCE
some strict advice   get   STROKEN
big luxury   GETOFFTHETELEQUICK
sis embarrassment   getluxurybuilding
harrassment   BIGLEADERTWICE
sis strict   KIDDINGYOURSELFYOUROBEY
some protect   SOMEBUILDINGPROVI
some correct   building   square   dial
sis brilliant   get off the page also
some embarrassment teacher   some silence
also   big disagreement   BUILDING
some officers   get LYING   BEWILDERED
some change   SUBJECTALTERITIVE
changes   HIS CHAIRQUICK
sis its funny quarrel   exit chair
some subject lounquit   have you said
big chair allowance said quick

title kick hard

sit silent teacher   obligated   dont rush it
many twelve   OBVIOUSHYSTERICALOBVIOUS
many quit   luxurious apartment
some   SILENTPROFESSOR   give lounger in
mother cheats   BIGLOUNGERBIG
someone closet   mother likes booking
just   CLOSETARRANGEOMIT   just paragraph
get closet end   GETSTRONGERTEACHER
mother   would   sit   STRONGER
mother object   much subject   illness
why be   CONTENTOBVIOUS   struggle
with advertise   SOMECOMPLIMENTS
mother gets strict advice silently on the
phone put it in article   practical
someone advertise   put it in   silently
put riquent fluent   some silent   comfusioneditorscramble
big hysterical   some combustion   gay where
put silent   get abovesilent   audiencequick
sis substructure should historical   mother
subject   OBNOXIOCAREFUL   quiet
sis at home   honest OBLIGATED   together
brother punishes   HISTORYHISTOROBVIJOKE
mother puts stronger in   strict silence

title kick hard

sis practice on people practice on people thats all it
says put it in   mother doesnt buy contaminated quit
products put it on the DANGERCEMENTpractical
put it in the   sis its just slightly above the line
youre reading   SILENTLYTELEQUIET silently
put it in the page correct   abstruction
sis containers obstruction   SILENTSIL
put it in the   obvious   mother practical
sis its silent subject   CONTAMINATED   get
off the screen   hannah mother hints   broke
economy   GETBREAKFASTPRODUCTS   many
sis youre   CONTAINERSEMPTY   shecomplete
mother would quit on this page inaminute
sis containers exam   PROFUSION
mother containers   sis products   poor brother
sis poor boxes   plenty excuse driving
get off the   mother hints excitement
mother explainslliterature   get history
writing   sis douglas office   put history
sis repeat protect   someone hints   get
suggestion   push button   sis scream
it up   big clean   embarrass elevatorman
big elevator   DRAWINGROOMpushbutton

title kick hard

my poor structure   is silence put
it historquit down   subsequence
honor   subject   contract   subject
getoffthepagesister   sis it just starts material
BIGOFFICEBIGFURNIUGLY   structure
write page   BEAUTIFULWOMAN
sis troublej   letterwriter   bravetypewriter
struck   COMPLETEDEDUCATION   promise
letter   JUSTTHEQUICKPROMISE   telephone
somelisten   subscribe   television
sis honor   TELEPHONEHISTORY   please
directory   give address   TRICKERED only
please admit   destory MATERIAL
confidsecretary   SOMEHISTORICALWRITING
enevlopes   scared   WITHOLDING
secret intelligence   sis its scared
writing   getscared   with profits
get witholding junk   perfect underletter
sis just TAXES   just employment
put it enjoy   SCAREDLETTERMENTION
secret offense   INTELLIGENCEPROFIT
put profit   get scared   INTELLIHOLD
sis scared withholding   taxes   opened
sis mother puts letter opened

title kick hard

put destroy   CONFIDENTIALWRITINGSCARED
sis scared   PROFITUNDERSTOPground
official   STOPINTELLIGENCE   quit profit
stop writing difficult   someone else quiet
sis writing   MATERIALPRIVATE   privatepublic
public listens   privatematerialwash
struggle   put historical   writingmaterial
put double   have you   CORRECTED   someone gets hunt
some   MATERIALSUBJECTCOMFORT   sis
just suggest   COMPANY   switch
just   SWITCH COMPANY   companion
put researcher   ENJOY COMPANION
some research get gay   LAUGHsubcomp
anion   hannah gets strict   have you ever
get LETTER   put lesbian   sister get gay off   between
put letter   subject   LESBIANWOMAN
put technique   WIFEput letter
put subject retreat   sameletteragain
put omit   have your strength   like
sis quit embarrass   WRITING some scared
sis just   POLITICALLETTER   forwardtome
hannah handsome   get off the formit page correct

title kick hard

sis secret INTELLIGENCE   PROVIDENCE
get hiding   mother likes writing a letter
put it on the page   SUBMIT   give a
blank surface   put historical big where   sis
correct   put it TWELVEPAGESLONGSICORRECT
providewhat   CITYPRESIDENTOFFICER
mother likes   PUBLICOFFScratch
getting   LETTERPROVIDENscratch   keeping
sit   remote   UNDERCONTROLMAGAZINE
mother TOUCHYCONTROL
big brother   sitday   sis just
control biglittle   BIGBROTHEROMITSADVANCE
give betterdinner   hannah
hints   local   big brother shutsit
sis forgive   letterwiriter   getstrict
some forget   BIGBORINGgetletter sis
it hints   providencespendingcorrect
boy are you boring   QUITLETTERWRITING
mother spelling   PUTDOUGLASIN   glasses
SOMETHINGELSEHOULDHAPPENacrossthepage
give twenty   ELEVEN   pageshurt
promise provicity   providencesomecorrect
mother would correct her page historical

title kick hard

put your brother in   sis put yourself under
BOSTON contract   put gradual   get gradual
big spelling   CORRECTSPELLINGGIVEADDRESS
sis skip   TWENTYPAGESembarrtechnique
on line   backwards   skip letter offending
mother lets SPENDINGSPENDINHIT
sis stretch   WOMANWONDERSWARNING
some subject   UNDERSTANDING
put subjectcompanionshipobstacle
sis   understanding perfect like quit
oh boy you poor perfect understanding
some people limit   subculture   sis hint
TELEPATHYstrong   UNDERSTANDING
between us   in the PUBLgivehint
get stricture   your office   telestroke
put telephone   TWICEGIVWIRING
mother   UNDERSTANDING   subunder
standing   culture   STANDINGHARD
letter screams   silent begintogether
sis put mother on the last page
and sign it   publishyourmateforget
sis scent   GETPUBLISHINGWRITE   sis sister
put publishing in after quit writing

title kick hard

sis quit lesson   put selfish one person
get instructions   from OTHER CLEAR
get perfect   ALWAYS INSTRUCTIONS
get office clear   keepclearoffice
say   TELEPATHIC   ordinary people
poor darling   SOME TELEPATHIC CONTROL
poor control   get center   controlcity
getwithstroke   get control   TELETOLD
sis suggest   TELEPATHIC   getting
control   clear at end   TRAVELAGABROAD
sis traffic   ORGANIZATIONS   puttrafficin
put sixteen   PAGESORIGIN   hint controlling
sis origin   TELEPATHIC CONTROL SAYING
mother puts   sis   embarrassing   contract
subscribe   INTELLIGENCECONTROLHINTING
mother argues   get strength only perfect
telecontrol   perfect office   some control
who writing   PUTATTHEEND sis
letter   public office   SCREAMING
someone hurts   sis its just a letter
screaming   put a letter screaming hurt
someone big telepathic   SPECIAL say print
dont hurt mothers perfect controlling perfect

title kick hard

obey puts letter in in a great big
organization getting PROFESSORSHIP
quit organization   SIS CONTROL
quit letter   quitorganization   mother lets
letter   put your ORGANIZATCONTROL
mother FINISHES SENTENCEONLY
paragraph just   UNDER CONTROL AGENCY
sisbigjoke   TELstrong   scrawl
OK intelligen put pretty   some organiz
sis control   PUBLICCONTROL   mother
thinks   FRIENDSHIP   quit historical
poor   FURNITURE   poorangellaughs
youre getting   PROVINCIAL   finish
sentence   STRUGGLEWITH   put letter squish
out of control   PUBLICAGENCY
put whisper in   SENDMATERIALput lecture
sis control   SUBJECTWRITING   get structure
mother sits   CONTROL PROVIDENCE
mother sug   get off telephone
mother likes material subject   get
off the line   SISTEREQUALPROMISE
sis lecture writing   special enjoy
sister get off enjoy   public audience
sis special subject enjoy submit enjoy

title kick hard

put your enjoyable   put your line in
sis   SKIP WRITING ENJOYABLE
mother would put another line
in say   enjoyable   SASPILL   the correct
Im writing   SPECIAL   INDIFTOLERANCE
scared   CHANGEPENSACRED   whatday
sis scared of it   write CHANGING
public   scared   PAsomequit   hurting
put handle in   SOMEPERSONALBEING
some children angry   likequarrel
quit   KIDDING ENJOYABLE   comfort
sis quit enjoyable   SEQUENTIAL   dont
destroy   LITERATURE   put it on ELECTRIC
sis destroy   TWENTYPAGESCOMPLETE
its a scanstronger   wordsomcrises
mother hints structure   STRANGERcomplete
sis its strong provstuck   BEWARE
get reading in   just beware kidding
get stranger political   youre YOUNGER
sis quilt excited   MANAGEMENT
pull telepsquare plug   IMPORTANT
put details   descriptionofput envelope scrawl
hannah it stuck   one line finished

title kick hard

overtwentconfused   mother likes   quit boy some space
likes writing   start page again   boys
hysterical   some writing   drop confidence
get quarter   seventy overfortypomit
some practice   unpubcomment   sequence
some practice   openly   COMMITTMENT
severe   DESTRUCTION   cityalmost
pray hard   boy HANDSOME   some
embarquit   HANNAH WRITING
sis public   mother intelligent   get
square   public overenjoyment
get gratitude   SIGLEEMQUIT
some english   SIDNEYAUSTRALIcontinue
sis it hurts   ENGLISHSPEAKING
desperately   MYomitsister
MYSISTERMYOMITSCAREDTODEATH
hangquarter   HANDSOMEBROTHER
some tragedy   sisteacherplease
some embarrassment   SCANDALS
some   COMMITTMENT   get politicalinstrcomplete understanding
tragic   big   sis serious accident   sis
scared finish   PARAGRAPH lot
sis finish page quickly   brother embarrassed
gives instructions on the last page thats all

title kick hard

sis some spending   quietly someone
sis urgent   his mothers correction
put struggle   INDEPENDENCE   calling
sis scriptintell   INDEPENcalling   mother only
scatter   sick   mother skips a phrquit
poor hycomfort   INDIPENDENstruck   shes
scared a little   someone else   object
catching   cold   night   obey window
instincts   JUSTIquarrel   obestrict
hannah   SOMEONEbreath   hannah
omit selfish   PERSONquiet
personal   SPELLING   correctspecorrect
always   PERSONALCOMMdestroy
sorry twenty sister   PAGESCOMMITTED
bank conomit   SOMEDESTROYCONsubmit
twist   special   HUNGRYABOUTindians
something   SPECIALalone   mother
ABOUThungrySPEallowakidding
sis   HANDLING   together
please pass   THEPAGhonest
give up   EXPERIENTIAL   TWICEbrave
sister control   PLEASEgive up altospace

title kick hard

brother puts you abastrict spellcorrect
sis strict luncheon   abroadinstrict
quit kicking   space   SOMEADVICEspent
sister keep writing instructions
one more how   INSTRUCTIONS
hannah youre giving up sbalance
thats plane   keep SILENCE   sis hint
breaking   your private   public interquiet
sis Im giving in public
strick CONFEspell   ONLY   mother
goes aboard a plane embarrass   sis mother
keep silence   strict   contract   amdance
sis punishment subject   get quarrel
mother keeps   AMBIVACONTquit
switch subject   keep plane abroad
hannah its   STRUCTURE   sit
put his   PUBLISHER   KEEP
STRUCambivalence   sickprowherehave
you been   STRUCK   subject be quiet
abroad silence   goes in it   keep twisting
sincere agonize   sissubjectEMBARRASSMENT
just finish   quit   sisculture
mother finishes page honest twenty

title kick hard

sis spelling correct should be the top
sis kindliness counts put it in
the subject scramble   consider article
pieces   SUBJECTALTEcorrect   discuss
abstract   PLENTY EDITORIAL squish
put subsequent in   some people embarrass
sis   COUNT   since article are written I
obey silence   QUITTING honest dear
say about knitting articlesmespcorrect
mother likes   FACTORYEMForgiquick
twenty give   HUNDREDGRANTED
sis engaged   put it in BACKquarrel
clairvoyantly written   INSOMEPAGEquit
hannah hints   STRUGGLE   put it in abstract
PUBLICPOLICYhint   some begin
PUBLISHCOUNTserious   pages hint
some historical   just seen like quit embarrass
material   WRITESUBJECTMATERIAL
mother PUTSINMATERIAL white
GREAT BIG content   switch it around
space omit   have speaking   PUBLICENERGY
HANNAH   ONEMORESERIOUS   PAGE
almost over   some silence
Hannah puts her name at the end signed silence

same page

SAME PAGE

sis struggle with indians first page should be the title

split charles laughs   infinitives   interlude
subject subject   ALTERITIVE   keep quiet people
charles has ugly   GREEN write same   interlude
put it in   SWEATER   sis its difficult
put in   STRANGE SWEATER obligated
sis we both   STRANGER   ugly meet
hannah hungry   stranger stranger
drink   INTERLUDE   official   finish period
where are   GREEN   WHITE   SWEATER
white pants interlude   sis its
given hint   public   STRONGER
put struggle   INDIANSWEATER   have
courage   put guess in   WONDERFUL
sis interlude   withCAREFUL
some indian   BECAREFULWITH
hint   STRUGGLEWITHINDIANS
sis   suggest indicative   problem
white   PANTS   he gets hint
livingroom   LIKE SWEATER
put in   LAUGHTER forgiven draw
daughweprovcity   becarefulwith
conclude wear   white
hannah I just sign my name put origin

SAME PAGE

lots of people much stronger than withitbe should be the title

subject alteritive   absolute put page two   absolute
integrity   indifference   SOME SUBJECT CONFERENCE
bruce plagerismforget   UPSTAIRSCONFERENCE provoke
subject sister   brave   BIG CITY   PROVICENTER
put mention names   SOME DELICIOUS   brave careful
slightly dangerous   have you CONFLICTED
some answer   DRUGGISTQUESTIONS   big words
sister page two   artificial respiration   holds
together   we sutear out this omit   subject above
similar   topic interference   big CAREFUL
instructor   big words   sis   ALTOGETHER
brother also   stop longer   bewildered
hurt name   ANDREWSSUBJECTSAMEOBJECT
some question   answer druggist pusher
some silence   INSTRUCTIONS   sis
instructor   be careful   INDIANSWITH
some sweater white   VERYCAREFULHEALER
thats subject get off hysterical   people enjoy
public gets hysterical   his writing
language   whos writing   ARTICLES
sis subject closed   SIGNHANNAHSUBJECTOFFICE   close

SAME PAGE

grant me subject should be the subject of my next title subject

handle it sandwiches   same SPREADING
writing   DIFFICU   complete ending story
youre furniture   once above   upstairs
be cruel office   getwithit   OFFICESTRUCTURE
some sublessflesconflictomit   SENTENCE
some beligerent   SOME BELL ABOVE
ring sequence   SOME SUBJECT INTERFER
compeducompleducompsenstrsitbealecturescare
my other   big   SISTER OTHERWISE
big official get off   OTHERWISE
give me subject   official   subjectotherwise
be careful with   hannah spell   WEINER
backwards   same gray INTELLIGENT
some subject intersubconobjegetquick
some interconflcontogconconferenobject
some apolowords   SOME CONFLICT
otherwise   SIT OTHERWISE   destroy
absoluconficstorconflobestory   OBEY CONFLICT
sis story   OBEDIENCESTRUGGLE with
opeconflict strugdoor   OMIT INTERFERENCE
put clear   put doorman   getconflictoverwith
sis its silently who together quick doorman seen

SAME PAGE
calling office struggle with sacrifice telephone

sis mother remembers   FRIENDSOMETEARS
when you were a small MOTHER
put it on paper   child   someone dies
grandmother   WELCOMEINARMS   sis
close   TOMYFOREVER believe
her tears   dries   TOGETHERFATHER
someday   PUBLICFOREVER
she STRONG   POWERFULOPENDOOR
tell doctor   SEE DIALAPROGRAM
hannah mother   winsanargument
dont dial   THETELEPHONEPHONE   some
answer   UNPOLITICALALWAYS   just
caress   DRINKHONEYTEA   somewhat
embarrassed   FORCEDRINKING   get drunk
sis I see instructions   keep me alive twice
so   I   CAN   LIVE   TWENTY   YEARS
so old   tiresome dies   SOMETIME
only   SOMETIME   that means
tenderness   SOMETIMESWORKING
on the   subtelle   gocrazytelephone
someone   INTELLIGENT   acrossthephone
silent   CRUEL UNDERSTANDING BELIGERENT   closing
sis paragraph   mother instead   brother closing
complete education   two pages official   contrast

SAME PAGE
argue title confuse article promise

public   some speak   some public   para
darling   discussed   argue subtitle
boy is he   DIFFICULTTOOBVIOUS
unpublic   TOPOFFICEJOKE   spell
correctly   hannah acupuncturist
understand parapsychology lecturer
written   some embarrassment   old friends
see your friend only   great office
put public enemy in   hannah some doctor
skip   UNTILNOVEMBERNOVEWHYCONSIDER
take name   SIS LINE   sis
just say   TELEPHONECOMPANY   sellabroad
comeonly   NEXTYEARSOMETIMEBEWARE thanksheroic
sis dont go   STRICTDIETSTRICTBREAD
please supply us confidence   omit
name DIRECTORSHIP   slight harrassment
obligated get off telephone quickest
slight attitude correct   attitude delicious
get off telephone   BEQUICKWITHSILENCE
mother   EMBARRASSMENT   put article
sincere APOLOGIES noa goes secret advertise
important   idiot   believe   TRICKERY
sit us silence honey   big enjoy keep silence
big brother only   sis just say clear obvious

SAME PAGE

some intelligent writer people should be my next subject put it on the page

dont joke this month   imposition   get article
letter   be   BETTERPREPAREDLETTER
some harrassment   sis drugs policeman
get off the EMBARRASSMENT   put in
wedding   repeat   WEDDINGPRACTICAL
so knows   KINDLINESS
kill intelligent   space INDICATED
put promotion in   KILL INTELLIGENT PEOPLE
address   somewhat ticklish   handle page
advance   strict   around   BIG HUNGRY
put EMBARRASSgetoffthepage
sis enough   somewhat embarrassment
I continue   special   PERFORMANCE
parapsychological   OMITOMITPARAGRAPH
class indeed   some confidence   some girl
twice   only two   PEOPLE HINT
get off the   HISTORICAL   some repeat
lesson   some historical embarquilt
SOMEONE ELSE SUBJECTIVE
big brilliant   CONFESSOR   sis quit
some writing   INDEEDCONFIDENTIAL
inclusorrysister   I write MYSELF
correct underwear   private some errors

SAME PAGE

sis subject should be your next title subject powerful

skip sentence altogether   big city
editor   PUTNEWSPAPERscrawl   big
city square   INSKIPCULTUSKIP
            MUCH BETTER PENMANSHIP
EXPERIENCE   author   skip practice
some marxism   PRACTICAL EDUCATION
give material   CITYCENTERNEWSCUT
give newspaper   OFFICIALMENT
sis skip forty pages   advise   advisor
mother likes me to quit writing please
sis   sentence style   SUBCULTUREOMIT
some subject   SISHISTORICLIBRCONTENT
mother   BIGOPENCITYLIKESTRONG
same   CITY   sis   backward keep clear
city   INTELLECTUALMANQUITPARADISE
special   JUSTMEETING   square clean
hannah popular education where
much publish   CENTRALCONTROLHUNGRY
bad intellectuals surprise   sweaters
sis give up   COLLECTINGADVERSHUTITFAST
must sculpture   giveuphintingculture
sis popular   AWKWARDADSCULPTURE
sis it means they comment advertisecareful sequence

SAME PAGE

dont you quit editorial writing change subject plus quaint literature

put in editorial   WRITINGREPEATSPECIAL
sis I know   WRITINGPROFESSQUIT   sis
quit   EDITORIALBOARDPROVINCIAL   sis
its   hannah you refuse to strategy
party   sis scream   PARTY OFFICIAL
dont hurt   SKIPSTRUCTUROFFICEquiet
put in your EDITORIALMANSHIP   sis
big eliminate   MANAGEMENTscream
skip   EDITORIALBOARDEMERGENCscream   PUBLIC
mother   EDITORIALBOARDPLEASE   pulisquit
some sentence   SUBJECTIVEOBEJECULOBJEHISTQUIT
hannah OBVIOUSWRITINGMANSHIP
sis quit   EDITORIAL   BOARDPOMQUAOMPLEASE
connectyoursentenpractiboarsequeforbiattractive
sentencestructure   gay   omit   say where
GIVECITY   sis scared   followpolicy
PLEASEPOLICYOMIT   quit quiet   GETTINGTWICE
big publisher   QUAINTCENTERCULHISTOPIC
sis submit   ARTICLESPROVIDE
mother lets me be finish structure
sis kid YOURSELFCWHEPROCIPUNCARRYOVERLOAD
sis last line   STRUCTURALMANSHIP

SAME PAGE

mother puts in another page in silence correct subject ignore

mother puts in joke   advise content
put in advisor   quit hinting agriculfinish
get off the quit   EMPLOYMENTAGENCY
just quit page   ELECTRICOMPANYBOSCONTROL
sis writing   PAGEINCLUDEDEDITORSUBCONTROL
mother born   where   give
date 1900 sacrifice   SPLENDIDARCHIVESPLENFSPELL
hannah editorial   BOARDSILENTPEOPLE
someone   INTELLECTUAL   substructure
silence   CULTURESERIESCONCERT
some cultural   subcultureprivate   sis
city   OBVIOUSWHEREcutitshort
some culture samecitysame
mother omits subject get off the allowance
intellectuals   SOMESUBJECTOFINCOLLECT
put subculture   CITYSTUCK
mother   SUBCULTURESTRUCTURE   office
just get home in time   get off office subject
be ashamed   get   EDITORIALCULTURE   just
omit   REPEATINGGETOFFTHESQUARE   sit
get off quit   embarrlaugh   LANGUAGEARTSUPPOS
quit writing seen employment historical board quit

SAME PAGE
please subject ILLUSIONMENT should be your title dont confuse people
some scared from illuminate city power title enjoy people are glad

just title exercise   put your back where
quit writing inde   just scared   please
hinting control   supervision   some quiet
independent   intact   sis Im quit agriculture
two more years   UNSTEADY CONTENT
sis agriculture   SAFETYATCONCERT
mother protects   ILLNESSCITYsome
verygreatagrispread   HANNAHIJUSTTEACH
people   JUSTEMPLOYSCREAMING
sisjustconnectyourwordssentenceomstruggle
putinyoursilenceperiod   SAMESUBJECTOSECRET
hannahalways   CORRECTSPELLkeepquiet
somecorrectspellconnectwordsforasentpage
hannah   people   should be struggle
justconnect   onemoregiveup   siscontrol
hannahImustntcontrocityomitindecorrect
omit subcuterror   OMITbig people
siscitycontrolcentergetoffconnect
mother controls   INTELLECTUALS
four pagescorrect   CONNECTEDMATERIAL
mother would someone is amusedcorrectsmile

SAME PAGE
sis subculture title interlude special attspell

hannah guarantee   officialdomcorrect
mother   corrects your penmanship   put it
onthepage   subculture   pagesconnectedpages
putitontheoffice   SUBPOSTSQUARE   TWICE
yourpoorcultureisobeyingitselfputitonthesilent
some   submit   page   TWICE   AGRI
sis submit correct   seqencesentencomplete
boys silence   instructor   education
sis promise city   promise compromise
big silent understanding   punishment cruel
subjective said objechard   said subjective twice
put it down in obey   plus title objeotherwise
mother hints subjective analysis
other person   bad habits drinking
sis culture quiet   culturaldrinkingsent
mother applies   gets job at the bar side
sis its agriculture were thinking embarrass
control it otherwise   put it down city
sis youre getting around aground   same
subject alternaswitcareful   strict control
same words   name committs   sis
quaint   same name control story
hannah Im the correct audience say word seen control
sis structure silence should be the end

SAME PAGE
slightly awkward title stupid on top squirrel page

same name omits providenceity same line continues
hannahIcanjustconnectmynamewordsbackwardsomitsentence
mother sincerity   big publisher destroy
confidential   destroy private comply editorial
very better languagecenterwriting   control obvious
I repeat literature   getoffthepageconnectwordssilent
sismotherwords   getprivatecompany   get
off   spell   connecting   WORDS HINTING
somewritingpublishable publishwritinghystermaterialcomment
mother publishes   OTHER publisher award hysterical object
hannah quaint bedding literature sissilent
sit silly   ALTERITIVE   please culture object
sis quaint literature should be omit organized
put publisher getting grant in specific putinhand
subject subject connectwords alteritavconnecembarrassconnect
publisher advertise please connect   please me connect
sis advertise control adjective   historical subject office
pleaseconnectwordsofficepresidentkidyourselfofficegetofftheconnect
pleaseconnectsubmerquaintliterconnecthequaintsisquaintliterature
sis holding back connectwordspublisherorganizeorganizecompliments

SAME PAGE
sis struggle with content should be contrseeobhanqucontroltwopages

mother puts struggle with indians in at the confuse title secure
some strong   like   same independent
some stronger women abroad driving
mother likes page sacrifice   hannah
have curtains   blouse   written in
have you any literature in your living
room that says boring   what laughter spell
put books   struggle with purple   on the
top   top squirrel office   some adverpolite
put your literature in on your shelf hispunish
hannah its welcome   walking period
some   soming   same people   hinting
like blank   dont say   last confessor
organize   put stronger material in public
guess   organization   make holler   somewhat
give page sublimit   have you iholler
give page a structure   sis struggle with
children with publish   struggle dont cancel
sis struggle with indians should be cancel
publisher wont let me spend any money
on teach blame   get off the publish
page correct   just publish your permit
sis language abroad struggle private
sis it   given in to it always   get indians in
hannah mother would last page correct
seen words with it should be in provide

Hannah Finegold Weiner was born in Providence, Rhode Island in 1928 and died in Manhattan in 1997. *Page* is the first posthumous publication of her work. The manuscript used for this edition was found among Weiner's papers, although she sent me an earlier version of the work on its completion in 1990. Both versions include the "Dear Hero" cover letter that precedes the text here. Most significantly, there were thirteen pages that were deleted from the earlier version of the manuscript. In this and all other respects, we have followed Weiner's later manuscript as closely as possible, refraining from making corrections.

Some biographical information may be useful in reading this work. Weiner graduated from Classical High School in Providence in 1946 and went on to Radcliffe College (1950). She grew up with both her parents and her brother; Weiner was the older "sis." While she was married for four years early in her life, she subsequently lived alone. From the time I met her in the mid-1970s, she would spend extended summers with her widowed mother and her aunt in her childhood home in Providence. Her mother died in September, 1984 and her aunt in January, 1985 and these events form the backdrop of the poem.

Hannah Weiner's books include *The Clairvoyant Journal* (Angel Hair, 1978), *Little Books / Indians* (Roof Books, 1980), *Spoke* (Sun & Moon Press, 1984), *Silent Teachers / Remembered Sequel* (Tender Buttons, 1993), and *We Speak Silent* (Roof, 1997). Her papers are housed at the Archive for New Poetry, Mandeville Special Collections Library, at the University of California, San Diego. Weiner's home page is located at the Electronic Poetry Center (epc.buffalo.edu).

Thanks to Lee Ann Brown, Patrick F. Durgin, and Susan Bee for editorial contributions to this book.

Charles Bernstein
August, 2002